EYEWITNESS BOOKS

BOOK

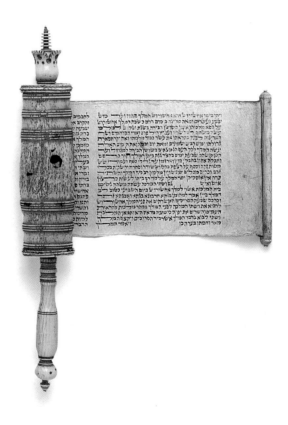

Steel-nibbed pen, made in imitation of a quill

Chinese calligraphy brushes

Chinese writing ink

Wax crayons

Remington

Selection of steel pen nibs

Early 20th-century typewriter

Ancient Roman pens and stylus

Mesopotamian cylinder
seal and impression

18th-century traveling
writing box

EYEWITNESS BOOKS

BOOK

Written by
KAREN BROOKFIELD

Photographed by
LAURENCE PORDES

17th-century
inkpot and
quill pens

16th-century book bound for King Henry VIII

Medieval
ink well

ALFRED A. KNOPF • NEW YORK

Thai folding fortune-telling book, mid-19th century

A DORLING KINDERSLEY BOOK

Project editor Phil Wilkinson
Art editor Ann Cannings
Managing editor Helen Parker
Managing art editor Julia Harris
Research Céline Carez
Picture research Kathy Lockley
Production Catherine Semark
Additional Special Photography Geoff Dann,
Nick Nicholls of The British Museum

This is a Borzoi Book published by
Alfred A. Knopf, Inc.

This Eyewitness ™ Book has been conceived by
Dorling Kindersley Limited and Editions Gallimard

First American edition, 1993

Manufactured in Singapore
0 9 8 7 6 5 4 3 2 1

Library of Congress Cataloging-in-Publication Data
Brookfield, Karen.
Book / written by Karen Brookfield.
p. cm. — (Eyewitness books)
Includes index.
Summary: Text and photographs trace the evolution of the written
word, how the alphabet grew out of pictures, the development of
papermaking, bookbinding, children's books, and more.
1. Books—History—Juvenile literature. [1. Books—History.] I. Title.
Z4.B78 1993
002—dc20   93-18833
ISBN 0-679-84012-5
ISBN 0-679-94012-X (lib. bdg.)

Color reproduction by Colourscan, Singapore
Printed in Singapore by Toppan

Page from a Qur'an written in Arabic script

Chinese woodslip

Chinese oracle bone

Modern clay tablet and stylus

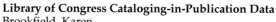

Early clay tablets

16th-century English book with embroidered binding and carrying bag

Anglo-Saxon styli for writing on wax tablets

Tray containing metal printing type

Contents

What is writing?

BEFORE THE DEVELOPMENT OF WRITING, people kept all their information in their heads. But it is difficult for human beings to remember everything and to pass it on accurately to someone else. Writing is a way of storing information and passing it on to other people who are some distance away in space or time. Writing was not invented by one person or even one society, but it evolved naturally in different places at different times from the need to keep accounts or to record events. It takes many forms, from simple picture writing to stylized scripts representing the sounds of a language, and it is found on every kind of material, from paper to pottery. Today, writing is an essential part of our everyday lives, not least in books like this one.

KEEPING TRACK
From the very beginning, writing was important for keeping records so that people were not dependent on memory alone. On this tablet from Mesopotamia, a simple drawing of an animal and a mark for a number told everyone how many animals there were.

MARKER
Writing has always been used to mark property and land, letting people know who the owner was. This terra-cotta marker is inscribed in a script called Oscan, which was used in Italy between the fourth and first centuries B.C.

LONG-LASTING
Before paper was invented, all sorts of writing materials were used. Pottery was readily available and cheap and lasted a long time. This piece has on it the text of part of a play by the ancient Greek dramatist Euripides written down about 2,000 years ago.

妙法蓮華經常不輕菩薩品第二十

爾時佛告得大勢菩薩摩訶薩汝今當知若
比丘比丘尼優婆塞優婆夷持法華經者若
有惡口罵詈誹謗獲大罪報如前所說其所
得功德如向所說眼耳鼻舌身意清淨得大
勢乃往古昔過無量無邊不可思議阿僧祇
劫有佛名威音王如來應供正遍知明行足
善逝世間解無上士調御丈夫天人師佛世
尊劫名離衰國名大成其威音王佛於彼世
中為天人阿修羅說法為求聲聞者說應四
諦法度生老病死究竟涅槃為求辟支佛者
說應十二因緣法為諸菩薩因阿耨多羅三
藐三菩提說應六波羅蜜法究竟佛慧得大
狼三昔提說應六波羅蜜法究竟佛慧得大
勢是威音王佛壽四十萬億那由他恒河沙
劫正法住世劫數如一閻浮提微塵像法住
世劫數如四天下微塵其佛饒益眾生已然
後滅度正法像法滅盡之後於此國土復有

WHAT IS A BOOK?
In China and Japan, many written texts take the form of a roll like this one. The Chinese script is written in vertical columns starting at the top right-hand corner. In the West, books have a totally different form, and the writing goes from left to right in horizontal lines.

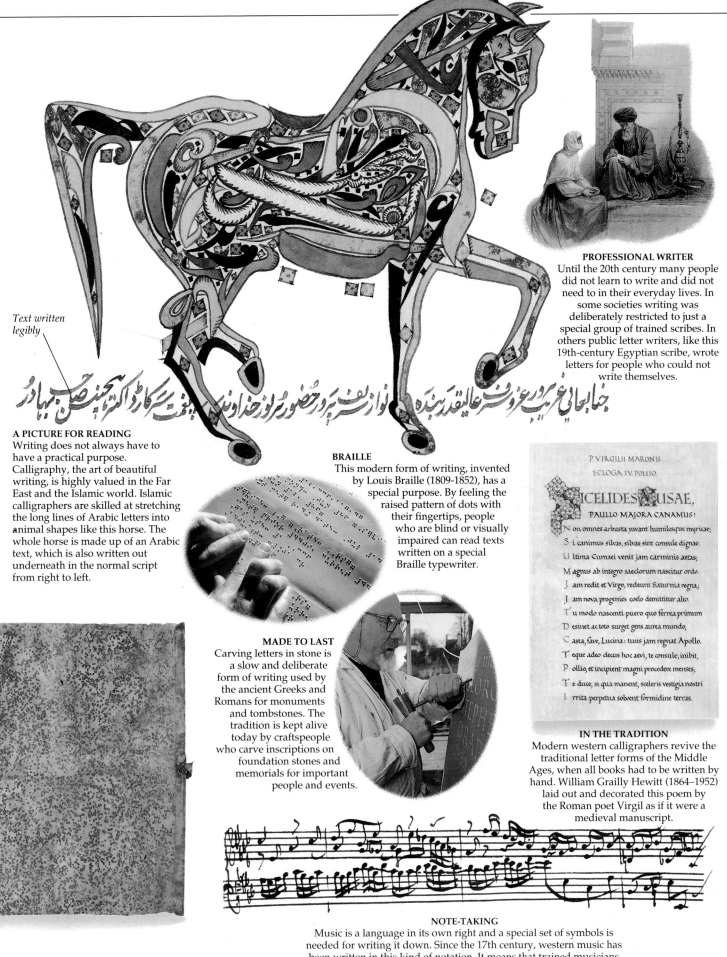

Text written legibly

PROFESSIONAL WRITER

Until the 20th century many people did not learn to write and did not need to in their everyday lives. In some societies writing was deliberately restricted to just a special group of trained scribes. In others public letter writers, like this 19th-century Egyptian scribe, wrote letters for people who could not write themselves.

A PICTURE FOR READING

Writing does not always have to have a practical purpose. Calligraphy, the art of beautiful writing, is highly valued in the Far East and the Islamic world. Islamic calligraphers are skilled at stretching the long lines of Arabic letters into animal shapes like this horse. The whole horse is made up of an Arabic text, which is also written out underneath in the normal script from right to left.

BRAILLE

This modern form of writing, invented by Louis Braille (1809-1852), has a special purpose. By feeling the raised pattern of dots with their fingertips, people who are blind or visually impaired can read texts written on a special Braille typewriter.

MADE TO LAST

Carving letters in stone is a slow and deliberate form of writing used by the ancient Greeks and Romans for monuments and tombstones. The tradition is kept alive today by craftspeople who carve inscriptions on foundation stones and memorials for important people and events.

P. VIRGILII MARONIS
ECLOGA IV. POLLIO.

SICELIDES MUSAE,
PAULLO MAJORA CANAMUS!

Non omnes arbusta juvant humilesque myricae;
Si canimus silvas, silvae sint consule dignae.
Ultima Cumaei venit jam carminis aetas;
Magnus ab integro saeclorum nascitur ordo.
Jam redit et Virgo, redeunt Saturnia regna;
Jam nova progenies coelo demittitur alto.
Tu modo nascenti puero quo ferrea primum
Desinet ac toto surget gens aurea mundo,
Casta, fave, Lucina: tuus jam regnat Apollo.
Teque adeo decus hoc aevi, te consule, inibit,
Pollio, et incipient magni procedere menses;
Te duce, si qua manent, sceleris vestigia nostri
Irrita perpetua solvent formidine terras.

IN THE TRADITION

Modern western calligraphers revive the traditional letter forms of the Middle Ages, when all books had to be written by hand. William Grailly Hewitt (1864–1952) laid out and decorated this poem by the Roman poet Virgil as if it were a medieval manuscript.

NOTE-TAKING

Music is a language in its own right and a special set of symbols is needed for writing it down. Since the 17th century, western music has been written in this kind of notation. It means that trained musicians throughout the world can read, understand, and perform this piece as intended by the composer, J. S. Bach (1685-1750).

First signs

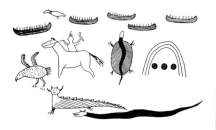

THE EARLIEST FORMS OF WRITING consist of sets of pictures of people, animals, and everyday objects. These are called pictograms, and the oldest known date from around 3000 B.C. To read this kind of writing you do not necessarily have to speak the same language as the person who wrote the pictograms – you just have to recognize the symbols. But it is easy to misunderstand a message or story. To record and pass on more complex information, societies developed ideograms, symbols that represent abstract ideas. For example, a picture of a pair of legs walking can mean "to go," or a starry sky can mean "night," "dark," or "black." The symbol may change its shape and look less like the real object it was based on, but it will still keep the same meaning.

HUNTER'S QUARRY
Some prehistoric peoples made beautiful paintings of animals, people, and abstract patterns on the walls of caves. These may represent creatures killed in the hunt and so could be a very early form of picture writing.

CHIEF'S JOURNEY
This North American rock inscription tells how a chief called Myengun went on a journey using five canoes. The trip took three days (three suns under a curved sky). The eagle is a symbol of courage, and the other creatures represent animal spirits that protected the chief on his journey.

BAD BOY'S SCROLL
Native North American peoples, such as the Ojibwa from the area around the Great Lakes, produced scrolls in which traditional stories were told in pictograms. This one belonged to a chief called Bad Boy.

MYSTERIOUS SCRIPT
left and right
The Indus people of northern India and Pakistan developed a writing system more than 4,000 years ago, but today we still cannot decipher it. There seem to be up to 400 different signs, which are used in inscriptions on seals like this one. The signs are mostly pictograms, but some are probably the names of people and places.

Indus seal

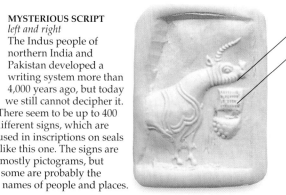

Bull

Signs

SEAL OF OWNERSHIP *below*
In ancient Mesopotamia (modern Iraq) people marked their property with cylindrical seals which they rolled along on wet clay to leave an impression. The pattern on a person's seal was like a signature. Seals were also used by traders because they were a quick and easy way to authorize contracts. Mesopotamian writing, on the other hand, was complex and was practiced mainly by specially trained scribes.

Impression   Goat

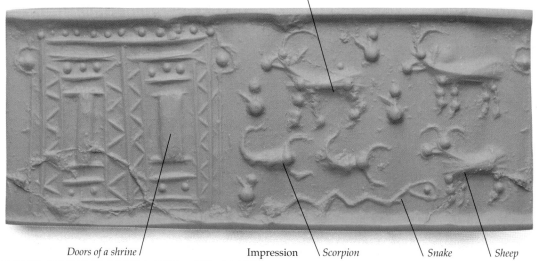

Mesopotamian seal made of gypsum

Doors of a shrine   Impression   Scorpion   Snake   Sheep

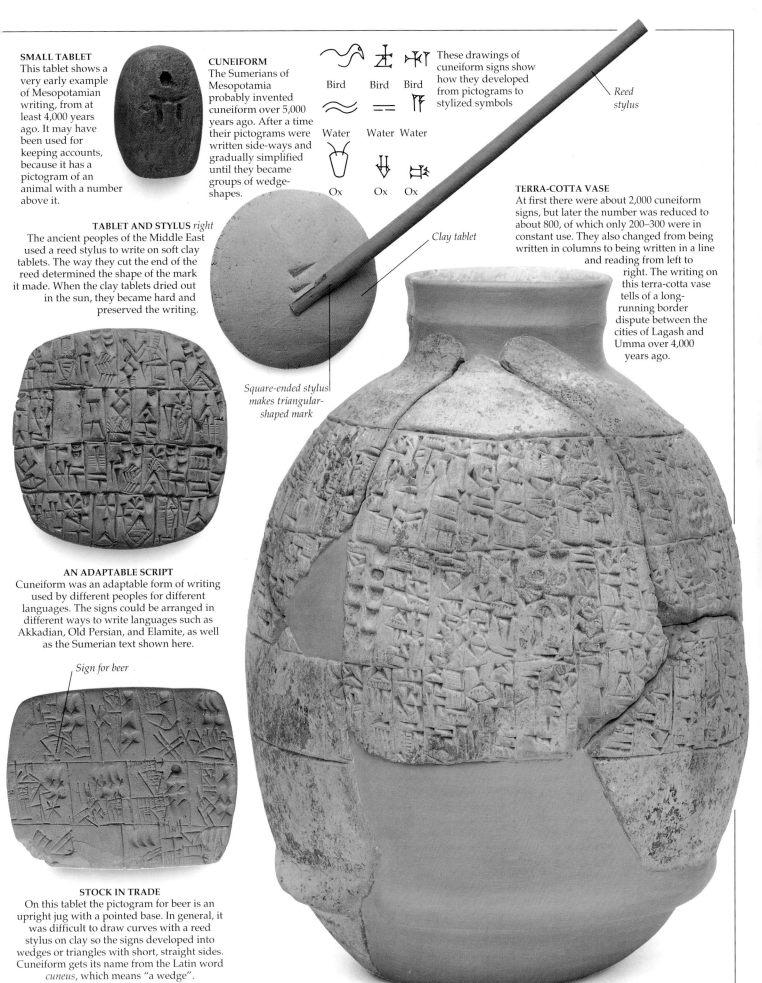

SMALL TABLET
This tablet shows a very early example of Mesopotamian writing, from at least 4,000 years ago. It may have been used for keeping accounts, because it has a pictogram of an animal with a number above it.

CUNEIFORM
The Sumerians of Mesopotamia probably invented cuneiform over 5,000 years ago. After a time their pictograms were written side-ways and gradually simplified until they became groups of wedge-shapes.

Bird   Bird   Bird

Water   Water   Water

Ox   Ox   Ox

These drawings of cuneiform signs show how they developed from pictograms to stylized symbols

Reed stylus

Clay tablet

TABLET AND STYLUS *right*
The ancient peoples of the Middle East used a reed stylus to write on soft clay tablets. The way they cut the end of the reed determined the shape of the mark it made. When the clay tablets dried out in the sun, they became hard and preserved the writing.

Square-ended stylus makes triangular-shaped mark

TERRA-COTTA VASE
At first there were about 2,000 cuneiform signs, but later the number was reduced to about 800, of which only 200–300 were in constant use. They also changed from being written in columns to being written in a line and reading from left to right. The writing on this terra-cotta vase tells of a long-running border dispute between the cities of Lagash and Umma over 4,000 years ago.

AN ADAPTABLE SCRIPT
Cuneiform was an adaptable form of writing used by different peoples for different languages. The signs could be arranged in different ways to write languages such as Akkadian, Old Persian, and Elamite, as well as the Sumerian text shown here.

Sign for beer

STOCK IN TRADE
On this tablet the pictogram for beer is an upright jug with a pointed base. In general, it was difficult to draw curves with a reed stylus on clay so the signs developed into wedges or triangles with short, straight sides. Cuneiform gets its name from the Latin word *cuneus*, which means "a wedge".

Writing with signs

CANG JIE
A Chinese legend says that writing was invented by Cang Jie, an official of the mythical Yellow Emperor, over 4,000 years ago. He created the script after looking at the patterns in tracks left on the ground by birds and animals.

WHILE EASTERN MEDITERRANEAN people were developing hieroglyphs and cuneiform script, the Chinese were creating a writing system of their own. The Chinese way of writing is a complex combination of pictograms, ideograms, and signs that indicate sounds. In all, there are over 50,000 signs – but fortunately for Chinese children and foreigners learning Chinese, you need only a few thousand for everyday life. Because the system used in China has changed very little during the 4,000 years of its existence, Chinese people today can read ancient texts without too much difficulty. The writing of some other ancient civilizations is still a mystery to us, despite scholars' efforts to decipher the texts that survive. It can take years of painstaking work to crack the code of a system that might at first glance look like simple picture writing.

Old — Child — Modern

Old — Tree — Modern

OLD AND NEW
The original pictogram can still be recognized in some of the modern Chinese characters.

Electric + shadow = Movie

MODERN IDEAS
Any new idea needs a new Chinese character – often a combination of exisiting characters.

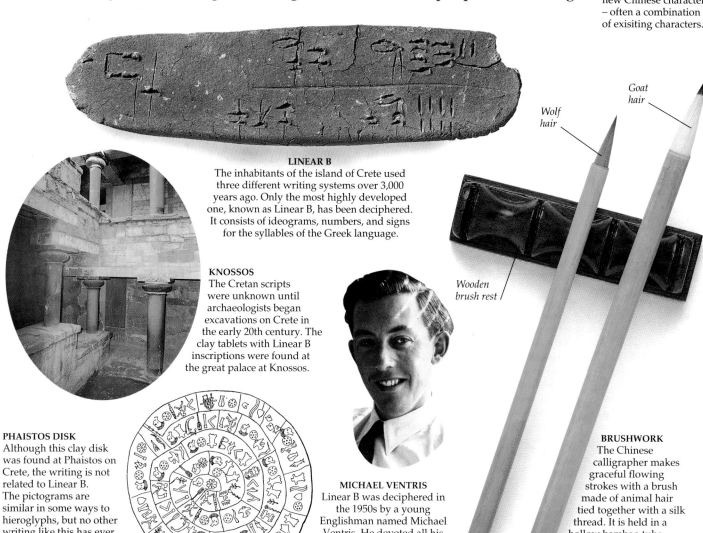

LINEAR B
The inhabitants of the island of Crete used three different writing systems over 3,000 years ago. Only the most highly developed one, known as Linear B, has been deciphered. It consists of ideograms, numbers, and signs for the syllables of the Greek language.

Wolf hair

Goat hair

Wooden brush rest

KNOSSOS
The Cretan scripts were unknown until archaeologists began excavations on Crete in the early 20th century. The clay tablets with Linear B inscriptions were found at the great palace at Knossos.

PHAISTOS DISK
Although this clay disk was found at Phaistos on Crete, the writing is not related to Linear B. The pictograms are similar in some ways to hieroglyphs, but no other writing like this has ever been found. The Cretans probably brought it back from a trading voyage to the eastern Mediterranean.

MICHAEL VENTRIS
Linear B was deciphered in the 1950s by a young Englishman named Michael Ventris. He devoted all his spare time from his job as an architect to showing how the script was used to write an early form of Greek.

BRUSHWORK
The Chinese calligrapher makes graceful flowing strokes with a brush made of animal hair tied together with a silk thread. It is held in a hollow bamboo tube. Chinese children have to spend a lot of time copying characters before they can write quickly and accurately.

PRACTICE MAKES PERFECT

Chinese characters are made up of as many as 26 different strokes which must be written in the correct order. This character, called Yong, which means "eternal," is the model character for practicing the five basic strokes. A famous calligrapher called Wang Xizhi is said to have spent 15 years perfecting his Yong.

First stroke

Second stroke

Third stroke

Fourth stroke

Fifth stroke

Black ink

Ancient characters

RULES AND REGULATIONS

About 2,000 years ago, Chinese government officials used wooden slats like this one to keep records. The characters look different from modern Chinese ones but can still be read. They are cut into the wood with a stylus or knife. This wooden slat shows which grade of soldier could carry messages and grain.

Characters carved into the bone

FORTUNE-TELLING

Some of the earliest Chinese writing is an attempt to predict the future. A heated poker was applied to an animal bone to make it crack. A diviner interpreted the cracks, in the same way that people read tea leaves today. The predictions about rainfall or the harvest or moving house were then carved into the bone, which can still be read today.

ONE PEOPLE, TWO SCRIPTS

The Hittites, from parts of modern Turkey and Syria, used two scripts – Babylonian cuneiform and their own pictograms. Before their culture died out they also developed signs for some of the sounds of their language.

MAYANS

The Mayans, who lived in Central America from 500 B.C. to A.D. 1200, developed two styles of writing for use on different materials. One was for carving in stone or jade; the other for writing on bark or deer skin. Their signs are pictograms inside squares or ovals.

PREFERRED MATERIALS

The best writing materials are those that are cheap, easily available, and do not need any special preparation. At first the Chinese wrote on wood, bamboo, and animal bones like this one. Later they used lengths of silk and paper, which they rolled up into scrolls.

THE RIGHT MIXTURE

Calligraphy is a highly valued art form in China and the right materials are all-important. Calligraphers mix their own ink by rubbing the solid ink stick into a few drops of water on the ink stone.

Solid carbon stick

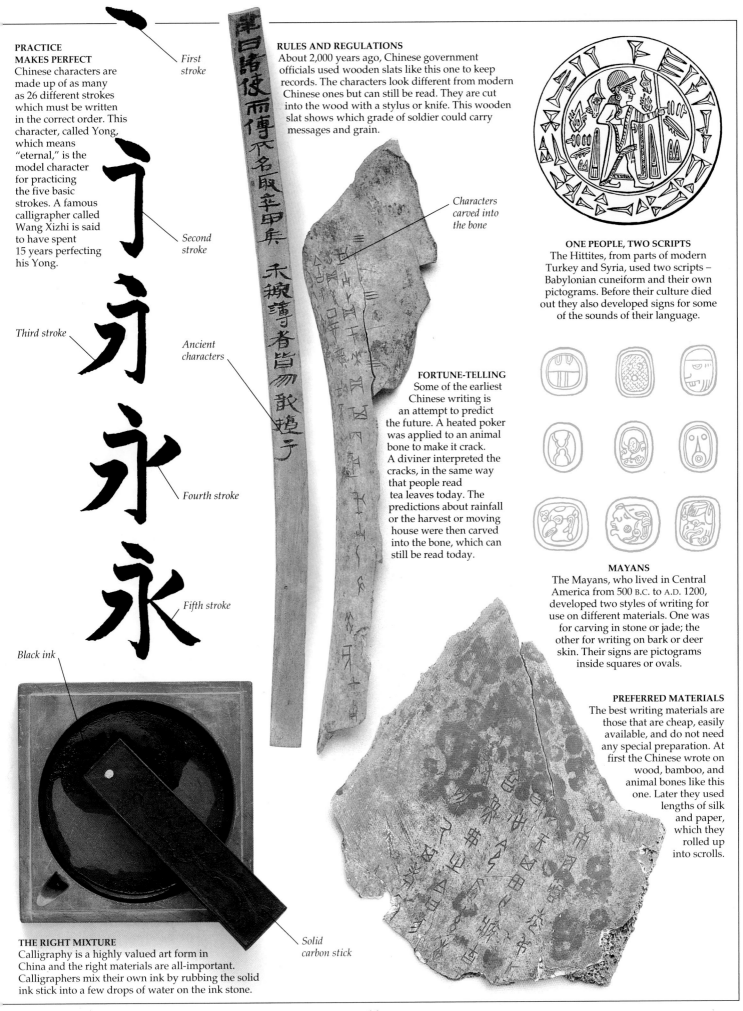

Egyptian writing

THE EGYPTIANS DEVELOPED a form of writing with pictures about 5,000 years ago. It came to be called hieroglyphs, from the Greek words meaning "sacred carvings," because it was used in temples, tombs, and other state monuments. At first sight, hieroglyphs look like simple pictograms, because they include many birds, parts of the body, and everyday objects. But they developed into a complex system where one hieroglyph can stand for a whole word in the Egyptian language or for just one sound. This makes some hieroglyphs similar to the letters of an alphabet. Writing hieroglyphs was slow, so gradually a faster form of the script, called hieratic, evolved, and later an even faster one, called demotic. At the end of the Egyptian civilization the Greeks ruled Egypt, so scribes had to master writing in a different way, with the letters of the Greek alphabet.

ROSETTA STONE
We would not be able to read hieroglyphs were it not for this stone. It is a thank-you to a ruler of Egypt with the text in three different scripts: Greek, demotic, and hieroglyphs. A Frenchman, Jean-François Champollion, deciphered the hieroglyphs by matching royal names in all three scripts and working out from his knowledge of Greek what the other symbols meant.

THE PROFESSIONALS
Writing in Egypt was practiced by highly trained professional scribes. They were rewarded well for this by having a very important position in society and special privileges, such as freedom from taxes. This scribe sits in the traditional position for writing.

Papyrus roll

MUMMY I. D.
This wooden label was attached to a mummy to identify it. The writing is in demotic script, which was always written from right to left. Demotic is descended from hieroglyphs, but it is almost impossible to see any resemblance.

Inkwell half-filled with black ink

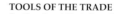

TOOLS OF THE TRADE
Scribes kept their brushes and pens in wooden cases, which they could carry around with them in case they had to travel. The black ink they used was made from charcoal or soot, and the colored inks – red, green, and blue – from minerals that were crushed and mixed with water.

Hieratic text

Cartouche

Hieroglyphs

DUCK DOODLE
Student scribes practiced drawing hieroglyphs on bits of pottery or stone called ostraca, which were cheaper than papyrus because they did not have to be specially prepared. Even once the young scribes were trained and skilled, they still had fun doodling in their spare time with some of the very elaborate hieroglyphs. This duckling was the word for "prime minister."

Hieroglyphs on temple walls could be carved directly into the stone, like this jackal

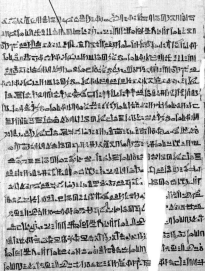

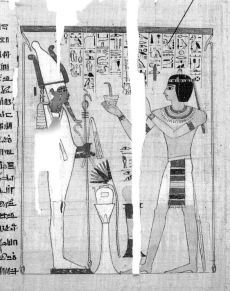

FROM HIEROGLYPH TO HIERATIC
Scribes needed a faster form of writing than hieroglyphs for letters and business contracts. The complex animals, birds, and objects were simplified into more abstract shapes in a flowing script called hieratic, which was always written from right to left. On this papyrus, hieratic is used for the main text on the left and hieroglyphs are used above the picture of a high priest making an offering to the god Osiris.

Eagle

Reed

Arm

Double reed

Chick

Leg

Shutter

Snail

Owl

Water

Mouth

Lion

REED PENS
For writing on papyrus scrolls scribes used thin reed brushes or reed pens. The reed is cut and split at the end to hold the ink. The reed pen was introduced to Egypt by the Greeks. Hieroglyphs on temple walls or statues were written with thick brushes made from papyrus twine.

COMMON HIEROGLYPHS
Hieroglpyhs could stand for a sound, as well as a whole word. For example, the mouth hieroglyph stood for the "r" sound, and the symbol for leg represented the sound "b."

ABC...

THE ALPHABET IS A DIFFERENT way of writing from pictograms or ideograms. One letter represents a sound in a language, and the letters are combined to make words. Today more people throughout the world use alphabets than any other form of writing. The alphabet is probably also the quickest and most efficient way to write. You need only 26 letters to write all the words in the English language. This makes the alphabet far easier to learn than 800 cuneiform signs or several thousand Chinese characters. We do not know exactly how or when the first alphabet developed, but it was probably invented by people living in Syria and Palestine around 3,600 years ago. The idea was passed on by traders, and different peoples developed alphabets for their own languages. Eventually this led to an extended family of alphabets, including the Greek, the Cyrillic, and the Roman, which is used for all the languages of western Europe today.

THE FIRST ABC
The people of Ugarit (in modern Syria) developed an alphabet to record the sounds of their language and used the cuneiform script to write it down. The alphabet has 30 letters and a special sign to divide one word from the next. Excavations at Ugarit in 1929 unearthed examples of the writing from over 3,000 years ago, including this tablet which is the oldest known ABC in the world.

PHOENICIAN WRITING *below*
The Phoenicians came from what is now Syria and Lebanon and were great sailors and traders. Their alphabet had 22 letters, and like other early alphabets from the same Semitic origins it left out the vowel sounds of the language. It influenced the development of other alphabets in the countries where the Phoenicians traded.

MESSAGE OF THE SPHINX
The earliest ancestors of the alphabet we use are Semitic alphabets developed by peoples on the eastern shores of the Mediterranean. These people probably knew about the other forms of writing used in the surrounding countries, but the alphabet seems to have been their own invention. They developed letters for all the consonant sounds in their languages but left out the vowel sounds. These would be filled in by the person reading the text. This sandstone sphinx from 3,600 years ago is inscribed in one of these early Semitic alphabets.

Inscription of the name of the goddess Ba'alat

GREEK ALPHABET
The Greeks learned the art of writing from the Phoenicians with whom they traded, probably about 2,800 years ago. They refined the shape of some of the Phoenician letters, changed some of the Phoenician consonants into vowels to suit their own language, and added extra letters for sounds that the Phoenician language did not have.

ΑΣΚΛΗ
ΠΙΩ
ΚΑΙ
ΫΓΕΙΑ
ΤΥΧΗ
ΕΥΧΑΡΙΣ
ΤΗΡΙΟΝ

Inscribed letters

ROUND AND ROUND
At first the Greeks wrote in almost any direction – even in a spiral, as in this inscription. The letter forms here are closer to the Phoenician than later Greek, and the writing is read from the outside toward the center. As the alphabet developed, the Greeks settled on writing from left to right and introduced spaces between words, as well as punctuation.

ΒΑΣΙΛΕΥΣΑΛΕΞΑΝΔΡΟΣ
ΑΝΕΘΗΚΕΤΟΝΝΑΟΝ
ΑΘΗΝΑΙΗΙΠΟΛΙΑΔΙ

TEMPLE INSCRIPTION
This Greek writing comes from a temple at Priene. The letters were finely carved in stone, with many strokes ending in short decorative cross lines that are known as serifs.

MENFRA

MENFRA

TURAN

TURAN

ETRUSCAN COIN
Around 700 B.C. the Greeks took their alphabet to Italy, where it was adopted and changed by the Etruscans. Short Etruscan inscriptions have been found on mirrors and other objects, such as coins, like this one made of gold.

ETRUSCAN WRITING
Etruscan was written from right to left. We can read it because many of the letters are similar to ours, but we do not know what all the words mean.

וכיראחילמלךכלהעלים
מעליכסוהננימעוהנאס
יהוהוהשבתיםאלהעיר
הזאתונלחמועליהולכדוה
ושרפהבאשואתערי

SQUARE HEBREW
This script has been in use for nearly 2,400 years with little change. The letters are written in an imaginary rectangular frame, which makes them very even. A system for adding vowels, as dots and dashes above or below the line, was developed when ancient Hebrew became extinct as a spoken language and it was feared that no one would know how to pronounce it properly with just the consonants.

ROMAN WRITER
Scribes were essential to keep the vast Roman Empire running smoothly, but they did not have the high social status of scribes in Egypt or Mesopotamia. Many were slaves of Greek origin. The well-educated citizens of Rome could read and write in both Latin and Greek.

Pointed stylus

Bronze pen

EARLY LATIN INSCRIPTION
At first Roman letters looked similar to Etruscan and Greek ones and were written from right to left, as on this very early Latin inscription. Gradually the shapes changed, some of the straight lines became curves, and the direction of writing was reversed.

WRITE ON
The Romans wrote on wooden tablets filled with wax, like the one this terra-cotta figure is holding. They also used ostraca (pp. 6–7) and papyrus (pp. 20–21). The papyrus had to be imported from Egypt, and they used so much that a shortage developed and new materials had to be found.

Reed pen

Flat end for erasing

PEN OR STYLUS?
As well as pens for writing on papyrus, the Romans used a metal stylus to inscribe their words into the soft wax of a tablet. When they no longer needed the writing, they rubbed it out with the flat end of the stylus and used the tablet again.

Phoenician	Modern Hebrew	Early Greek	Classical Greek	Etruscan	Classical Roman	Modern Roman
𐤀	א	A	A	A	A	A
9	ב	B	B	8	B	B
𐤂	ג	Γ	Γ	Γ	C	C
◁	ד	Δ	Δ	∩	D	D
𐤄	ה	Ǝ	E	Ǝ	E	E
Y	ו	⅃		ᴀ	F	F
					G	G
I	ז	I	Z	I		
⊟	ח	B	H	𐌇	H	H
⊗	ט	⊗	θ	⊗		
Ɀ	י	⟨	I	I	I	I
						J
Y	כ	K	K	K	K	K
ι	ל	Λ	Λ	J	L	L
M	מ	M	M	ᴟ	M	M
Ϻ	נ	Ͷ	N	M	N	N
‡	ס		Ξ	⊞		
O	ע	O	O	O	O	O
𐌓	פ	Γ	Π	𐌓	P	P
~	צ	M		M		
φ	ק	φ	Ρ	φ	Q	Q
◁	ר	𐌓	P	◁	R	R
W	ש	⌇	Σ	⅄	S	S
†	ת	X	T	T	T	T
						U
		Y			V	V
						W
			Φ			
			X		X	X
			Ψ			
			Ω			
					Y	Y
					Z	Z

THE ALPHABET FAMILY
When the Romans conquered the Etruscans, they took over the Etruscan alphabet and adapted it to their own language. Some letters that the Etruscans had derived from the Greeks were not used, and new letters were added. The Roman alphabet is essentially the same today as it was 2,000 years ago.

INKS FOR WRITING
Like many other peoples, the Romans made their ink from soot mixed with water.

INK POTS
Roman writers kept their ink in clay or stone pots like these.

SQUARING UP
Carving in stone requires careful planning to make sure that all the words fit in and are properly spaced. Roman draftsmen used a square like this to keep the outlines straight.

MONUMENTAL LETTERS
In stone inscriptions the Romans used only capital letters, though they developed other styles for everyday writing. The carver first drew the inscription with chalk and then painted the letters with a brush. The sweep of the brush gave the letters their shape and made thick and thin strokes. The stone carver followed the same line when carving out the letters with an iron chisel.

Wreath of laurel leaves

Bronze stylus for writing

Carved letter M

Thick and thin strokes

COMPASS
Each letter fits inside an invisible square or circle so that the characters are regular. The Romans used compasses to draw circles. Sometimes you can see marks made by compasses in the centers of rounded letters.

17

ANCIENT SOUTH ARABIAN

This script was used in parts of the Middle East between 500 B.C. and A.D. 600, when it died out. Not many examples of it survive, but there are some monumental inscriptions and bronze tablets like this one. South Arabian script used 29 letters representing only consonants. One version of this script developed into classical Ethiopian and the modern Amharic scripts of Ethiopia.

Runic inscription

ANGULAR ALPHABET

Runes were used by Scandinavian and Germanic peoples between A.D. 200 and 1200. There were usually 24 letters in the alphabet, but the Anglo-Saxons, who used it in England, added extra letters for the sounds of their language. The angular characters have very few curves, probably because they were first carved in wood or bone, and carving curves would have been difficult. Runic inscriptions have been found on monuments, weapons, charms, and other objects such as this whalebone casket made in about A.D. 700.

ARABIC SCRIBES *above*

These scribes wrote in Arabic script, which is written from right to left, and was probably first used in the late fourth century A.D. It became much more widespread with the revelation of the Islamic faith three centuries later (pp. 34–35).

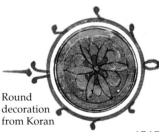

Round decoration from Koran

ARABIC

Although the Roman, Hebrew, and Arabic scripts look very different, they can all be traced back to the same early developments in writing. Like Hebrew, Arabic started as a consonantal script – readers were expected to add the vowel sounds as they went along. Later on, vowels were indicated by extra marks above or below the letters.

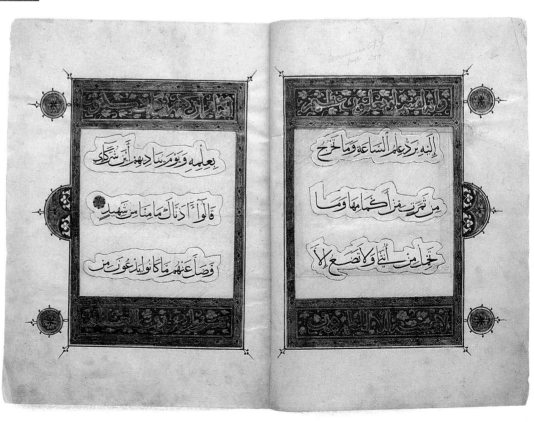

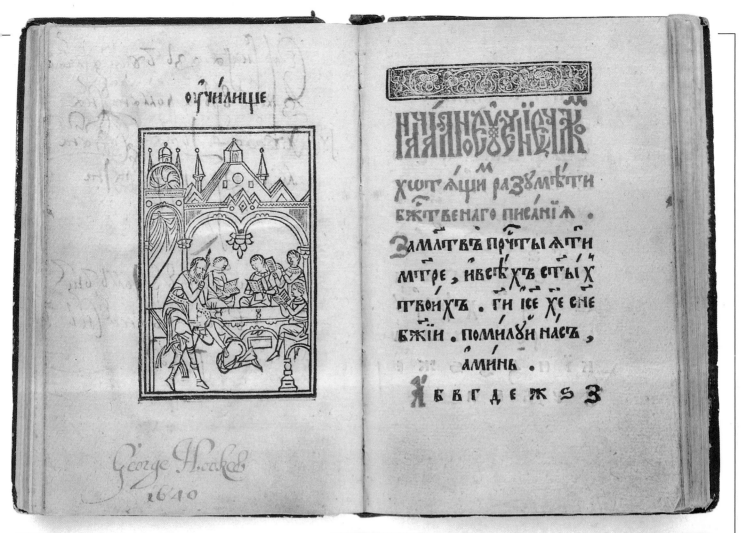

CHURCHMAN'S SCRIPT
The Cyrillic alphabet used in Russia is named after St. Cyril, a churchman who preached the Christian faith to the Slavic peoples. This book is a 17th-century textbook for an old form of the Russian language, Old Church Slavonic, printed in Cyrillic script. At the time there were no printed grammars of modern Russian, so language students used this book to learn Russian.

WOODBLOCK DECORATION
The decorative panel at the top of the page was printed using a woodblock.

HEAD OF THE PAGE
The heading of the page of the Old Church Slavonic textbook is written in a script called Viaz'. It developed from an old habit in manuscripts of writing the first line of a text in larger letters than the rest. The letters are joined and entwined to make a decorative pattern.

А	Л	Ч
Б	М	Ш
В	Н	Щ
Г	О	Ъ
Д	П	Ы
Е	Р	Ь
Ж	С	Ѣ
З	Т	Э
И	У	Ю
І	Ф	Я
Й	Х	Ѳ
К	Ц	Ѵ

CYRILLIC LETTERS
The original Cyrillic letters were based on the Greek uncial script of St. Cyril's time, the ninth century A.D. The Slavic peoples of Russia, Bulgaria, Serbia, and other countries took up the Cyrillic script.

Ꭰ	Ꭱ	Ꭲ	Ꮶ	Ꮻ	ꭵ
Ꮝ	Ꮖ	Ꭹ	Ꭺ	Ꭻ	Ꭼ
Ꮧ	Ꮲ	Ꭿ	Ꮀ	Ꮐ	Ꮿ
Ꮃ	Ꮞ	Ꮲ	Ꮆ	Ꮇ	Ꭷ
Ꮵ	Ꮊ	Ꮒ	Ꮂ	Ꮥ	

INSTANT ALPHABETS
A number of scripts were invented in the 19th century for languages that had not previously been written down . These included African and native North American languages. A Cherokee called Sikwayi invented this alphabet for his language between 1820 and 1824. Only some of the 85 letters in the alphabet are shown here.

In addtion to the Cherokees, other Native American peoples, such as the Crees, invented new alphabets

19

Before paper

ONCE PEOPLE START TO KEEP written records of trade, agriculture, and major events, they need a constant supply of material to write on. They can use natural materials, such as wood, bamboo, or bone, but these are difficult to write on and are not practical. The ancient Egyptians found that they could make an excellent material for their documents from the papyrus plant. The knowledge of how to make papyrus sheets spread all over the ancient Mediterranean world. When the supply of papyrus began to run out, people looked for a substitute. The result was parchment, which was made from animal skins. Until paper reached the West in the Middle Ages, parchment was the most important writing material.

PLENTIFUL PAPYRUS
Papyrus for writing on is made from the stem of the papyrus plant. Once the ancient Egyptians had learned how to do this, they had a cheap and plentiful supply of material for all their written records. The earliest surviving papyrus is over 5,000 years old. The Egyptian state controlled the production and trade in papyrus, from which it made a lot of money.

Bushy top

Triangular stem

PLANTS WITH A PURPOSE
Papyrus grew in large plantations in the valley of the River Nile, but so many plants were needed for writing materials that eventually they became scarce. Papyrus was also wasteful because only one side could be written on.

LAYERING
After the stem has been cut from the papyrus plant, its green outer rind is removed and thin strips are cut from the white inner fibers. The strips are laid out side by side, edges overlapping. Another layer is put on top across the first. The layers are pressed or hammered so that eventually they stick together with the plant's own moisture. When they have dried in the sun, the sheets can be written on.

Inner fibers

Green outer rind

LONG ROLLS
Scribes stuck sheets of papyrus together to form long rolls. This ancient Greek papyrus is nearly 13 ft (4 m) long. The text is written in narrow columns so that it can be read easily, one column at a time. Papyrus was an excellent material for rolls, but it was not good for a bound book because it tended to break up when the pages were turned many times.

Overlapping strips

PRODUCING PARCHMENT

The animal skin is first washed in clear water and then soaked in a solution of lime for up to 10 days. Both sides are then scraped to remove any remaining hair and flesh, and the skin is soaked again. It is then stretched on a wooden frame like this one and scraped with a curved knife. When it is dry, it is scraped again to make it as smooth as possible.

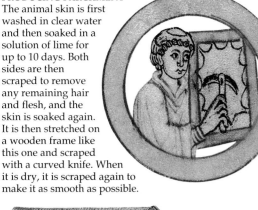

PARCHMENT FOR SALE

By the 15th century, scribes could buy rolls or sheets of parchment in shops like this. One man is trimming a skin into rectangles the shape of pages; the other is rubbing a sheet smooth with a stone.

LEATHER GOODS

Parchment is an altogether different kind of material from papyrus. Like leather, it is the skin of an animal, usually a sheep, goat, or calf, but it is treated to make a soft, smooth surface for writing on. Legend says that parchment was invented by King Eumenes II of Pergamum (197–158 BC) because he could not get his usual supply of papyrus from Egypt, and the word parchment comes from Pergamum. It is more likely that the material developed gradually from the ways of tanning leather.

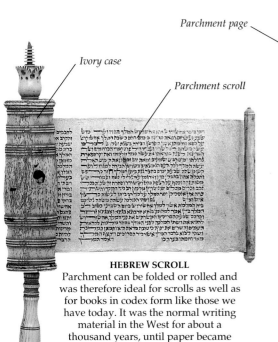

Parchment page

Ivory case

Parchment scroll

HEBREW SCROLL

Parchment can be folded or rolled and was therefore ideal for scrolls as well as for books in codex form like those we have today. It was the normal writing material in the West for about a thousand years, until paper became widely available. Even today important documents like certificates are sometimes written on parchment.

Handle to hold scroll

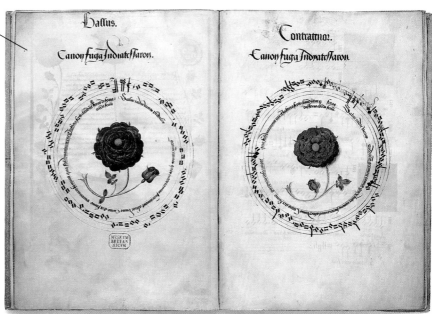

MUSIC FOR A KING

The two sides of a sheet of parchment are different. The side that was the hair side of the animal is darker and creamier than the side that was the flesh side. When the sheets are made into a book the facing pages always match. This book written on parchment contains music written in honor of King Henry VIII of England over 450 years ago. The words and music have been written around in a circle because it is to be sung in canon (as a round).

Paper

FLOWERY
Paper from southeast Asia sometimes has flowers and leaves pressed into it.

HIGH DEMAND
Once printing was established in Europe, the number of books produced increased enormously, and so did the demand for paper. In the 19th century, papermaking machines were invented. Cotton and linen rags were becoming scarce and expensive so wood was introduced as the new raw material for machine-made paper.

TRADITION SAYS that paper was invented in China by Cai Lun, an official of the Emperor He Di, in the year A. D. 105. The Chinese kept the process of making paper a secret for 700 years until Muslims invading Samarkand captured some Chinese prisoners who passed it on. Eventually the knowledge spread to Europe, and paper mills were set up wherever there was a good supply of water for making the pulp. The best paper is made from plants that have a lot of cellulose in their fibers, or from rags made from natural materials such as cotton or linen. The Chinese found paper cheaper to produce than silk and more convenient to use than bamboo or wood slats, especially for long books. In the West, paper replaced parchment as the most common writing material.

MATERIALS FOR PAPER
The Chinese used mulberry bark or bamboo to make paper; the Europeans used linen and cotton rags. These were beaten in water to make a pulp.

PAPER MOLD
The essential tool for making paper by hand is a mold for scooping up the soggy pulp. This Japanese mold is quite elaborate, with a hinged wooden frame to hold the mesh in place. The papermaker dips the mold in and out of the vat and gently shakes it to settle the pulp on the mesh. The clips are then opened and the mesh lifted out. A Western mold has fine wires instead of the bamboo mesh.

VATMAN
When the vatman puts the mold into the vat, the pulp collects on the mold and the liquid runs through, leaving a thin layer of fibers.

THE SQUEEZE
The fibers form a sheet of wet paper. The sheets are piled up and the water squeezed out with a boulder or with a press rather like a printing press.

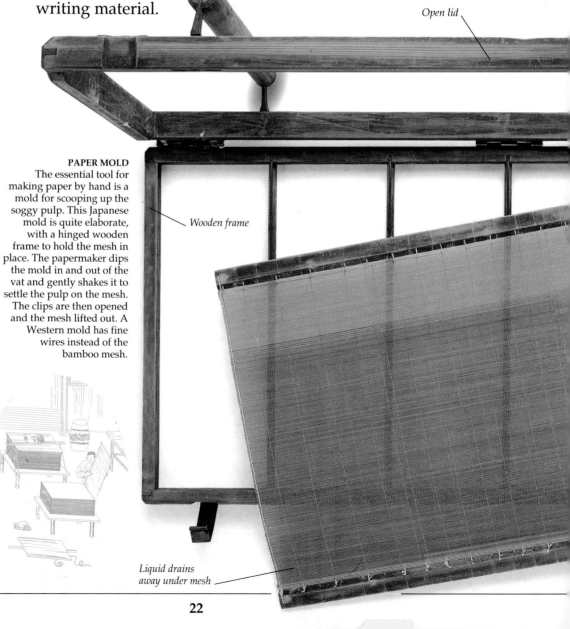

Open lid

Wooden frame

Liquid drains away under mesh

IN COLOR
Islamic papermakers were the first to dye, or color, their papers. They even speckled them with gold or silver. Nowadays paper comes in every color imaginable. Special paper like this might be used for a diploma or certificate.

PAPERMAKERS IN ACTION
After the rags have been beaten into a mushy pulp, the vatman dips the mold into the huge vat containing the pulp. He lifts out enough to make one sheet. The next worker places felt over the soggy sheet of paper to squeeze out the water and puts the sheets under the huge press. Two more people remove the felt when the paper is dry.

Handle to grip while dipping mold into pulp

THE MARBLER'S BENCH
Marbling is done by dropping blobs of colored paint into a tray containing a mixture of water and a moss, dragging a comb across the surface to make the colors swirl in patterns, and then laying a sheet of paper on top to pick up these patterns.

THE MARBLER'S ART
The Chinese and the Persians knew how to marble paper hundreds of years ago. In the West marbled papers are often used for lining the inside covers of books.

Tattered, yellowing page

REMY DE GOURMONT

Le
Problème du Style

LE PROBLÈME DU STYLE
LA NOUVELLE POÉSIE FRANÇAISE. — QUESTIONS D'ART.
LA LANGUE FRANÇAISE ET LES GRAMMAIRIENS.
LA DISPUTE DE L'INDIVIDUALISME.
NOTES ET COMMENTAIRES.

AVEC UNE PRÉFACE ET UN INDEX DES NOMS CITÉS

Nouvelle édition

PARIS
MERCVRE DE FRANCE
XXVI, RVE DE CONDÉ, XXVI

SELF-DESTRUCTING PAPER
Paper made from rags is strong and lasts a long time, but modern paper made from wood pulp does not. It turns yellow, crumbles, and finally disintegrates altogether because it contains a lot of acid. In only 60 years a modern book can end up looking like this.

Clip to close mold

Bamboo mesh

A medieval Psalter

I<small>N THE MIDDLE AGES</small> it took a long time and cost a great deal of money to produce a magnificent book like the one shown here. It is a Psalter, a book containing the words of the Psalms, for use in Christian church services and in private prayer. Rich people who wanted to show how wealthy and important they were paid scribes and artists to make illuminated manuscripts like this just for them. This Psalter was made in about 1315 for a rich person associated with the town of Gorleston in eastern England, so the book is now known as the Gorleston Psalter. The words of the book, over 500 pages, were copied out carefully and beautifully by hand by just one scribe; the decoration was done by as many as six different artists.

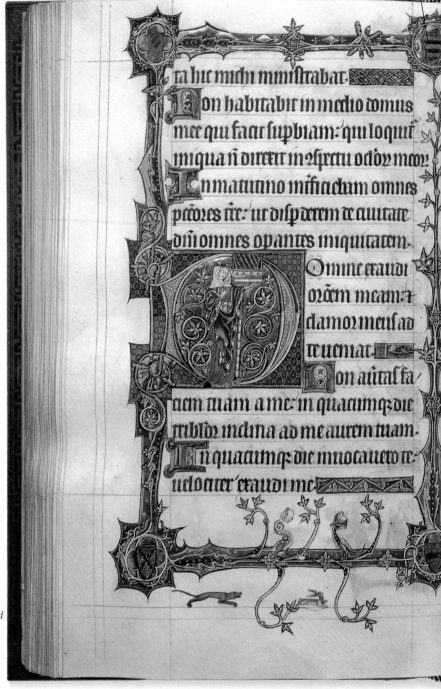

Coat of arms

Initial D

Figure of a woman

Patterned background

AT THE BEGINNING
The beginning of Psalm 101 is marked by a large initial letter D with a picture and an ornate pattern inside it. The text was written first and the decoration added later, so a space the right size was left for the letter.

GOTHIC SCRIPT
The book is written in Latin in a style of writing called Gothic book script, which has very angular and very regular letters.

Initial letter N

Gothic book script

Human head on bird's body

GROTESQUE
Artists drew many strange creatures, called grotesques, with human heads on animal bodies.

LET THE DOG SEE THE RABBIT
The margins of the page are filled with pictures of real and not-so-real scenes. The dog is chasing the rabbit along one of the lines drawn on the parchment when it was being prepared for writing (pp. 20–21).

WELL PRESERVED
Although the book is nearly 700 years old, it is in excellent condition and the colors are still bright and fresh.

Grotesque

Coat of arms

FLOWER BORDERS
Trees, plants, and flowers provided the inspiration for much of the border decoration. Such plants were also used in making the artists' paints.

CLUES TO THE PAST
We do not always know when or where a manuscript was made. Sometimes there are clues in the book to help us, like these coats of arms, which belong to families from the Gorleston area.

Bird

Line filler

FILL UP THE PAGE
When the words did not reach the end of the line, the space was filled in with patterns, birds, or animals. A different artist did this kind of decoration from the one who did the initial letters and the other pictures.

Line filler

Geometric pattern

Gold leaf

COLORS OF THE RAINBOW
Artists often had to make their own colors from plants or stones, which they ground up. The finest deep blue was made from lapis lazuli, which came only from Afghanistan. Artists also used real gold leaf, which they stuck to the surface of the parchment with gum.

Knight on horseback

Grid lines provide guide to position of words and pictures

HUNTING A MONSTER
Some medieval manuscripts have pictures of the person who had them made. We do not know definitely who commissioned the Gorleston Psalter, but perhaps he was a knight like this one. He must have been rich because he had to pay the scribe and the artists for their work and materials.

Winged monster

Acorns and oak leaves

Manuscript books

DECORATED LETTERS
Many medieval books are illuminated. They frequently have large decorated initial letters to start pages or chapters in the Bible. There is often a small picture inside these letters.

As IT MARCHED across Europe, conquering region after region, the Roman imperial army brought with it the Latin language and the Latin alphabet. The peoples of western Europe adapted the alphabet to the sounds of their own languages and changed the forms of the letters to create different national styles. Often these styles were developed by clergymen, and many books were made for the Christian Church, which needed a lot of Bibles and other books for use in its services. Monks in monasteries made magnificent illuminated, or decorated, manuscripts to reflect the glory of God. Not everyone could read or write, but as more and more people learned, they too began to demand books for their everyday life. Until printing became possible in the 15th century, every single book had to be written by hand.

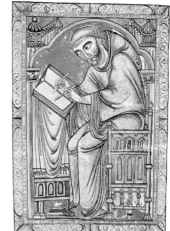

EADWIN
Eadwin was a monk at Canterbury, England, who drew a picture of himself in a Psalter (book of Psalms). Around the edge of the picture he wrote in Latin that he would be remembered forever through his writing.

Flat end for rubbing out

Point for writing

Stone to sharpen knife before cutting quill

ANGLO-SAXON WRITING TOOLS
As well as writing on parchment, the Anglo-Saxons also used tablets filled with wax for notes and for planning the layout of large books. They wrote on the tablets with a metal or bone stylus that had a pointed end, and they rubbed out the words with the flat end. Writing on parchment is easiest with a hard quill pen (pp. 56–57).

Metal clasp holds book closed and keeps parchment curling

BOOK OF HOURS
Individuals wanted small books for private prayer. A book of hours was a special kind of prayer book that was a medieval best-seller. When the book is closed, the clasps hold the pages together.

TWO SCRIPTS

The Europeans found that writing on parchment with a quill pen altered the style of their writing. At first they used capital letters all the time, but later they developed faster styles with small letters. The Latin text of this Psalter is written in uncials, which are rounded letters. There is also a translation into Old English between the lines of Latin that is in a different script.

FIT FOR A KING
Books made for kings and princes often included a picture of the scribe presenting his work to his patron.

Musical notation

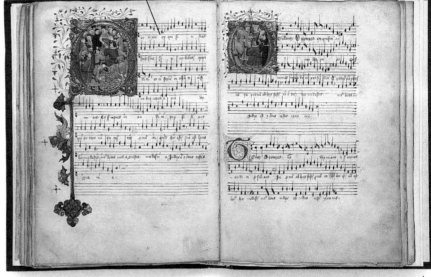

WRITING MUSIC
Musical notation developed about a thousand years ago when marks like these were written above words to be sung in church. They were intended to remind the singers of what they had learned by heart.

CAROLS
By the 15th century, music was written on lines to indicate how high or low the notes should be sung. Scribes used the same materials for music manuscripts as for other kinds of books and decorated them in the same way. This book of carols was made for use in the royal chapel at Windsor Castle, England.

Explanation to help reader

Latin text of Bible

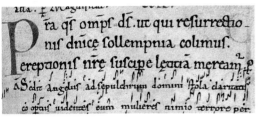

Notes written above the words

Illuminated letter P

MEASURING UP
Part of a scribe's skill was to fit all the words of the text on the pages of the book without huge gaps and without wasting expensive parchment. First the scribe measured the page, marked out the area he could write in, and ruled guide lines. He left a space for the illuminated initials, which were filled in after he had copied out the words. A text like this, in four columns, required particularly careful planning.

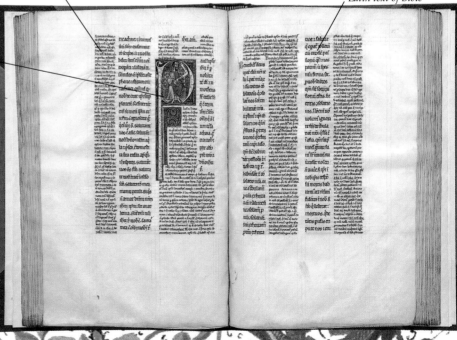

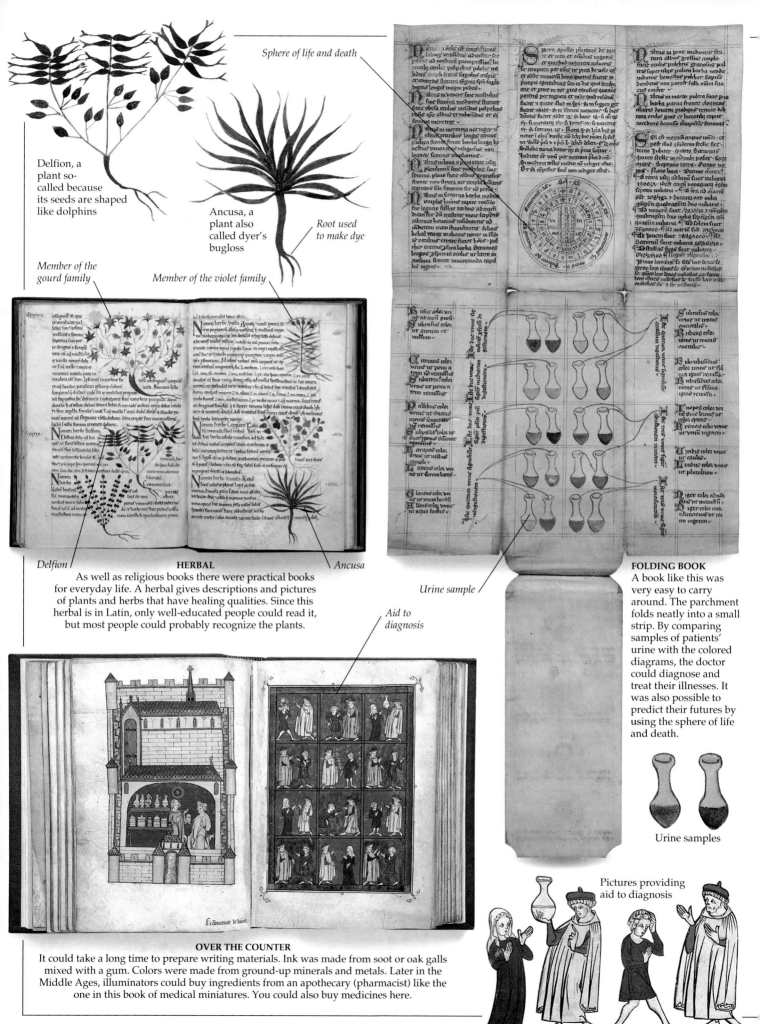

Delfion, a plant so-called because its seeds are shaped like dolphins

Sphere of life and death

Ancusa, a plant also called dyer's bugloss

Root used to make dye

Member of the gourd family

Member of the violet family

Delfion

HERBAL
As well as religious books there were practical books for everyday life. A herbal gives descriptions and pictures of plants and herbs that have healing qualities. Since this herbal is in Latin, only well-educated people could read it, but most people could probably recognize the plants.

Ancusa

Urine sample

Aid to diagnosis

FOLDING BOOK
A book like this was very easy to carry around. The parchment folds neatly into a small strip. By comparing samples of patients' urine with the colored diagrams, the doctor could diagnose and treat their illnesses. It was also possible to predict their futures by using the sphere of life and death.

Urine samples

Pictures providing aid to diagnosis

OVER THE COUNTER
It could take a long time to prepare writing materials. Ink was made from soot or oak galls mixed with a gum. Colors were made from ground-up minerals and metals. Later in the Middle Ages, illuminators could buy ingredients from an apothecary (pharmacist) like the one in this book of medical miniatures. You could also buy medicines here.

RED INK
Scribes used red lead, the mineral vermilion, or even crushed kermes beetles to make red ink.

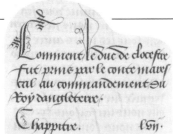

SWIFT OF HAND
Froissart's Chronicle is written in French in a spiky script called Secretary that is fast to write and easy to read.

Words written in Secretary script

SCRIBE AT WORK
Many illuminated manuscripts have pictures of scribes. Here medieval scribe Vincent of Beauvais sits at a desk, pen and knife in hand, poised to begin work. Not all medieval books were made by monks. Later, professional scribes based in towns copied books to order. They had to be able to write in a variety of scripts to suit the book – and the customer.

FLOCK OF SHEEP
The most expensive materials for making an illuminated manuscript were the gold for the decoration and the parchment for writing on. Each double page of a large book needed one sheet of parchment, which meant one animal skin – or a whole flock of sheep for just one book. The 14th-century Frenchman Jean Froissart wrote a long and lively account, called a Chronicle, of events in Europe in the late 14th century. The Chronicle was copied many times in books like this.

Paper strip with text

Handle

BY ROYAL COMMAND
Kings and other rulers employed clerks to write letters for them and to keep a record of their reign. When the king gave orders to the people, the clerks had to write them out many times to be sent to all parts of the country.

Decorative border from Froissart's Chronicle

IS IT A BOOK?
This world history is one of the most curious "books" ever made. Notes in German on events from the Creation to 1595 were written on long strips of paper. The writing is clear, but there is no obvious beginning or end.

Books from Asia

FOR NEARLY 2,000 YEARS the usual form of book in the western world has been the codex – large sheets of paper folded down the middle, grouped together in sections, and bound between covers. In other parts of the world the book has taken very different forms. You can write on just about any kind of material – natural or artificial. Tree bark, bamboo, cloth, silk, palm leaves, and even ivory have been used and made into books. Bark can be rolled into a scroll; palm leaves can be strung together so that you can find any particular leaf quite easily; sheets of paper as long as 33 ft (10 m) can be folded like an accordion.

IVORY
Ivory from the tusks of elephants has always been a rare and expensive material. In Southeast Asia it was used for sacred writings and for special letters to very important people. This letter was written in 1858 in thick gold paint on seven sheets of ivory. It was sent in its own ivory box. It is written in Burmese script.

PALM LEAVES
Palm leaves provide the most common writing material in India and Southeast Asia. Because they are fragile and easily destroyed by damp and insects, not many very old palm leaves survive. These are from the 18th or 19th century. Before a leaf can be written on, it has to be cut to the right size, soaked, boiled in milk or water, dried, and rubbed smooth.

Blade for scraping surface of palm leaf

Wooden board

Palm tree from Southeast Asia

Palm leaves with decorated edges

STRUNG TOGETHER
A palm leaf book is not sewn together like a western book, but held together by two cords threaded through holes in the middle of the leaves. A wooden board, like a cover, is attached to the top and bottom of the pile of leaves to protect it. The edges of the 498 leaves in this book have been gilded and painted with red lacquer.

Decorated wooden board

STYLUS
Scribes used a bronze stylus like this to write on palm leaves.

JAPANESE TALES
This Japanese book was originally made in the form of a scroll. It has been converted into an oblong book with pages by folding the book like an accordion. The folds can be seen along the book's outer edge. Both Chinese and Japanese books are made like this because the paper used in them is fine and delicate.

ON YOUR METAL
Because palm leaves are so perishable, legal and religious texts were sometimes inscribed on metal plates. This Buddhist text is written on copper in Burmese square characters.

BAMBOO
The ancient Chinese and some later peoples wrote on strips of bamboo. These 19th-century strips are from Sumatra in southeaast Asia.

Writing was carved with a knife before being blackened to make it stand out

CHARACTERS
The Japanese language belongs to a different language family from Chinese, but the Japanese adapted Chinese characters so that they could write down their spoken language. Japanese children learn 881 characters in their first six years at school. Like Chinese, Japanese is written in vertical columns from right to left with a brush and ink.

HELP AT HAND
This little booklet is about 1,000 years old. It was designed to help in emergencies. It contains part of the Lotus Sutra, a Buddhist prayer, in Chinese. If you are set upon by thieves or caught in a fire or flood, you recite the prayer and call upon a spirit to help you. It is much easier to open a booklet at the right place than to open a scroll.

SILK HAND-KERCHIEF
Most books are too big to hide up your sleeve in an exam, but this piece of silk, the size of a big handkerchief, is the perfect crib sheet. It contains 94 model answers written by people who passed in the Chinese civil service exams in the 19th century.

Decorative border

INDIAN SCRIPTS
Knowledge of writing came to India with Semitic traders about 2,500 years ago. Today there are about 200 different scripts in use. This 18th-century book is written in the Sarada script from Kashmir, northern India.

BARK SCROLL
This tiny 18th-century scroll is written in an Indian script called Devangari.

Mara, spirit of evil

Decorative cover

CUTTING YOUR CLOTH

This book is made from the cloth of monks' old robes. The cloth has been cut into rectangles (the shape of a palm-leaf manuscript) and stiffened with black lacquer. The letters are inlaid with mother-of-pearl. The book is a sacred Buddhist text. It was written in square Burmese script, probably in the 19th century.

Horse

Rooster

FORTUNE-TELLING

Folding books are traditional in Thailand as well as Burma. They are made of long sheets of heavy paper made from the bark of the khoi bush. This 19th-century book is a guide to telling fortunes using the Chinese horoscope. Each year has an animal sign, and the animal is shown in four different positions for different parts of the year.

BUDDHA *right*
Buddhism originated in India, and as it spread to other parts of Asia so did its sacred writings. The script of the Indian Buddhist monks was adapted by other people for their languages.

FOLDING BOOK
In Burma folding books called parabaiks often tell the story of the life of Buddha in words and pictures. Reading from left to right, this book tells of Buddha's meditation, his defeat of Mara, the spirit of evil, and Buddha's enlightenment. A decorated cover protects the book when it is folded.

Islamic books

THE ARABS WERE ORIGINALLY nomadic peoples who had little need for writing in their everyday lives. But in the early 7th century, a great change occurred with the revelation of the Islamic faith to the Prophet Muhammad. The word of God was revealed directly to Muhammad and then had to be written down by his followers to ensure that it was always passed on correctly, because the word of God should never be altered. The holy book of Islam, the Koran, is therefore in Arabic, the language of the Prophet, and it is in Arabic script. Muslims the world over read and recite the Koran in Arabic, whatever their own language may be. Arabic script can also be used to write languages other than Arabic itself in the same way that the Roman alphabet is used for many different languages.

EASTERN KUFIC
Kufic script developed different forms in different countries. Eastern Kufic, from Iran and Iraq, has slender, graceful lines. This page is from a Koran copied about 1,000 years ago. The red and gold rosette marks the end of a verse.

WRITING FROM A WALL
The Koran teaches that the art of writing is a gift that God has bestowed on humans. As well as its practical use in giving information in books, writing is used as decoration on all kinds of objects. When Muslims worship in a mosque, they can see writing all around them. Texts from the Koran are often found on tiles, like this example from a mosque in Isfahan, Iran.

Text from the Koran

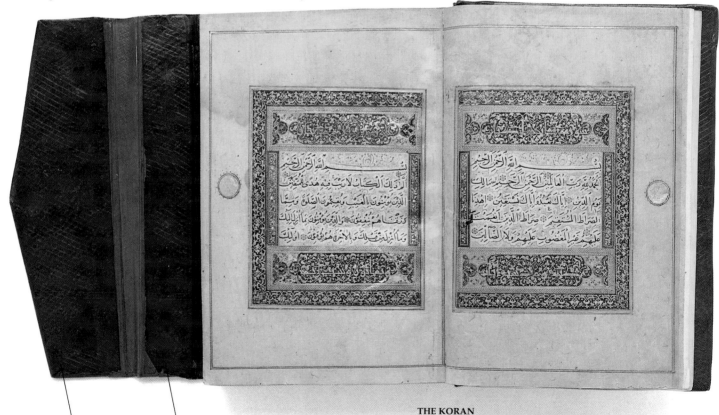

Flap to protect the book

Original leather binding

THE KORAN
Muslims believe that the Koran contains the words of God exactly as they were given to the Prophet Muhammad. Scribes strive to convey the word of God as perfectly and as beautifully as they can. This Koran was copied in Turkey about 500 years ago in Nashki script, which is now the script most frequently used for the Koran.

THE WONDERS OF CREATION

Arabic script is used for all kinds of books, not just Korans. Although the Koran has no pictures, only decoration composed of patterns and the letters themselves, other books such as this treatise on the creation of the universe do have illustrations.

ISLAMIC SCRIBE

The Islamic scribe traditionally sits on the floor to write and uses a reed pen which he trims with a knife. He is highly regarded in Islamic society, especially if he devotes himself to writing out the Koran.

MARK OF THE SULTAN

Each Turkish sultan adopted an elaborate monogram, called a tugra, to bear his name and to be his official signature. It was used on coins and buildings as well as documents.

Nasta'liq script

Decorative border

FIT FOR A PRINCE

The decoration on the borders of this page is made up of stylized flowers and leaves. The book is richly decorated throughout with many large pictures and was probably made for an important person like a prince.

BOOK OF KINGS

The Persian language is written in Arabic script. This copy of the Persian national epic poem, called the *Book of Kings*, is in a graceful script called Nasta'liq. Legend says that the calligrapher who created this script modeled the shape of his letters on the wings of a flying bird that appeared to him in a dream.

Getting ready to print

PIONEER OF PRINTING
German goldsmith Johannes Gutenberg (c. 1400–c. 1468) is credited with inventing movable type about 550 years ago. He found a way of making large amounts of type quickly and cheaply. The idea spread rapidly throughout Europe.

FOR CENTURIES, THE ONLY WAY to produce a book was to write it all by hand. Even with many scribes working together, only a small number of books could be made. There had to be a quicker and cheaper way to satisfy the ever-increasing demand for books, but the Europeans were very late in discovering it. Printing was invented well over a thousand years ago in the Far East, almost certainly in China, but was not adapted for use with western scripts until the 15th century. The Chinese printed scrolls and books using wooden blocks with whole pages of characters carved into them. The greatest advance for western printing was movable type – a single letter on a small block that could be set into words, lines, and pages, and re-used many times.

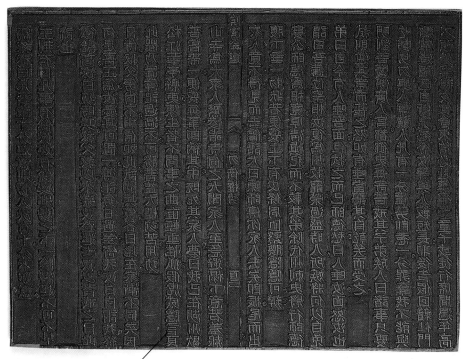

Chinese characters in reverse

CHINESE WOODBLOCK
The Chinese used blocks of pear or jujube wood for printing. The text of one or two whole pages was first written out by hand in ink and then laid face-down on top of the block. The block was then cut so that the text stood out in relief and in reverse. The printer spread ink over the block and pressed a sheet of paper down on it to leave an impression of the characters the right way around.

BLOCKMAKERS
These Japanese blockmakers are cutting a wood block to produce a result similar to the Chinese block shown on the left. They are using a mallet and chisel to cut the shapes in the wood.

Unfinished letter

FIRST STEPS
The first stage in printing with movable type is to design the shape of the letters. Gutenberg based his letters on the writing of German scribes. These pattern cards show the attempts of an Englishman, Sir Charles Wilkins (1749–1836), to design type for Marathi, a language using Indian script.

Marathi letter in ink

Notes on the Marathi letter

TYPE FOUNDRY

Movable type is made from a mixture of tin, lead, and a bluish-white substance called antimony poured into a mold by a worker called a typecaster. A skilled typecaster could cast 4,000 letters in a day – that is, one every 10–12 seconds – but only the best could make each one perfect. Type often came out uneven, making it useless for printing.

IN BUSINESS
Many different craft workers were involved in the process of making perfect type for printing. This man is using a plane to shave off rough parts after the type has been cast.

MAKING PUNCHES
The first step in casting metal type is to make a punch out of hard metal. Using the drawings of the letters of the alphabet as a model, each letter is carved in relief on the end of the thin stick of metal so that it stands out.

USING THE PUNCH
The typecaster next hammers the punch into a small block of soft metal, such as copper, to leave an impression of the letter.

MATRICES
The piece of soft metal with its impression of a letter is called a matrix. This is put into a mold and held tightly in place. Hot molten metal is then poured into the mold until it is full to the top.

PIECES OF TYPE
When the mold is opened the piece of metal type can be removed. One matrix can be used to make many identical pieces of type.

MODERN MATRICES
These matrices have been made recently from the old punches shown on the left.

BOX OF TRICKS
This box contains a set of matrices for casting type for the Marathi letters on the pattern cards opposite. The box lay unopened for 140 years after Sir Charles Wilkins's death in 1836. The people who made the matrices for Sir Charles used exactly the same processes as Gutenberg's workers several centuries before.

ॲ ऍ ओ ठ अ म ऍ
उ ढ ण न थ ट घ
प ज ष त च ह ।
म ॲ क्त क्र क्ष ध ॉ
त्त त्र घ ध्र म ॉ न
म ऊ म ठ ष्ठ ॉ प
ई ह ट ु ब ट ट श

PROOF THAT THEY WORKED
When Sir Charles' matrices were discovered, they were used to cast type and the type was used to print a specimen on a hand press.

Typesetting

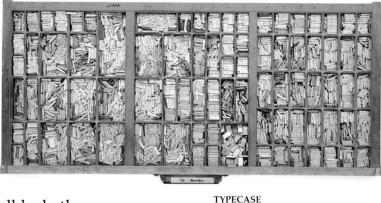

Once the printer has acquired a set of type, the actual printing process can begin. One of the advantages of movable type is that mistakes can be more easily corrected than with woodblock printing. If a Chinese printer made a mistake when carving a woodblock, the character had to be cut out and replaced with another, which might not fit properly. The printer with movable type can easily substitute one letter for another without any loss of quality. A printer's reputation rests on the finished work, so printed text is checked carefully at every stage.

TYPECASE
A traditional printer stores type in a wooden tray called a typecase. For each letter of the alphabet there are three sorts of type: capital letter, small capital, and small letter. There are also numbers, punctuation marks, and spaces – making up about 150 different sorts in all. Each has a compartment of its own in the typecase.

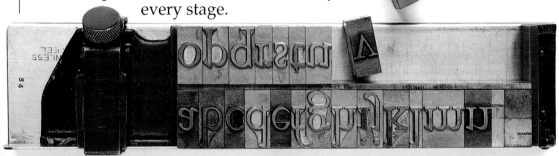

1 COMPOSING
Putting type together for printing is called composing. The compositor picks out type from the typecase and arranges it on the composing stick. The grip on the left can be adjusted to give the correct length of line. The first printers used wooden composing sticks, but later metal ones were introduced.

2 THE WORLD BACKWARD
Here is the Roman alphabet in capital and small letters of two different sizes. The size of a typeface is measured in points: the bigger size is 24 point; the smaller, 12 point. In the composing stick the letters read from left to right, but they are upside-down and back-to-front so that they will eventually print the right way around.

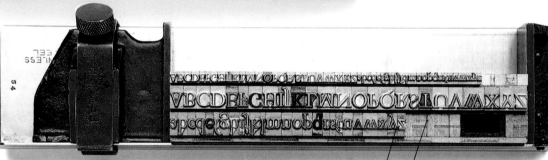

24-point type

Leading

Block of type being transferred

Composing stick

THE CAREFUL COMPOSITOR
The compositor must always take care to pick the right letters from the case. A mistake here can mean an error when the book is printed.

3 STEADY HAND
When the stick is full, the compositor carefully lifts the block of type out and puts it on a larger tray called a galley. One slip of the hand can ruin all the work.

4 GALLEY
Spaces between blocks of text in the galley are filled with solid metal pieces called leading. They are lower than the type and so do not print.

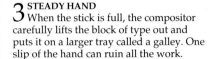

60-point type

Special forms of letter fit neatly together

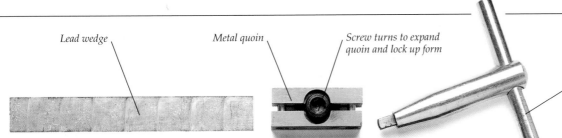

Lead wedge

Metal quoin

Screw turns to expand
quoin and lock up form

Quoin key to
turn screw

Quoin key

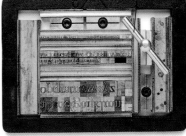

6 TIGHTENING UP
A final turn of the key locks the
form. It is now virtually a solid
slab. None of the type, leading, or
furniture should drop out when it
is lifted, even though it does not
have a bottom.

Metal quoin

5 CHASE
When all the type is ready, it is moved from the galley to an
iron frame called a chase. The spaces between the type and the
chase are filled up with wedges known as furniture. The chase,
type, and furniture together make up a form. Originally the
wedges were wooden, but later metal ones were used.

Printers
put ink on
the form
using a
leather ball
stuffed
with
horsehair

GUTENBERG'S WORKSHOP
Johannes Gutenberg must have been proud of the
first perfect sheet printed with his new invention,
movable type. He had come up with a simple idea
that transformed the way books were produced.

abcdefghijklmn
opqrstuvwxyz

abcdefghijklmnopqrstuvwxyz
ABCDEFGHIJKLMNOPQRSTUVWXYZ

ABCDEFGHIJKLMNOPQRSTUVWXYZabcdefghijklmnopqrstuvwxyz

RED-LETTER DAY
This is what the upside-down, back-to-front
alphabet looks like when printed in red.

7 INKY FINGERS
The form is now ready for inking and then printing. The
water-based ink used by medieval scribes was not suitable
for printing, as it could not be spread evenly over the type.
So printers developed an oily ink made with nut or linseed
oil; a pigment based on soot gave a rich deep black.

Raised type

On press

JOHANNES GUTENBERG PRODUCED the first page printed with movable type in the German town of Mainz in the 1450s. He built a wooden press with a screw mechanism like those of the presses used in crushing grapes to make wine. This pressed paper against raised type (pp. 38–39) covered in ink so that the type made an impression on the paper. The news of Gutenberg's success spread very rapidly around Germany and into the nearby countries. By the end of the century there were printing presses in almost every country in Europe. For the next 400 years or so, printers used presses of the same basic design as Gutenberg's, with wooden presses being replaced by iron ones, which were stronger and lasted longer. In the 19th century the hand press was superseded by machines for mass production. But the finest printing is often still done by hand.

WILLIAM CAXTON
The first English printer was William Caxton (ca. 1422–1491). He learned the new craft in Cologne, Germany, and printed his first book in Bruges, Belgium. Later he returned to England to set up a printing shop in London.

EVERY PICTURE TELLS A STORY
Some early printed books have pictures. The image was carved in reverse on to a woodblock and the block put into the form (pp. 38–39) with the type. This is a picture from Chaucer's *Canterbury Tales*, printed by Caxton in 1483.

LIKE A MANUSCRIPT
The first printers wanted their books to look like the beautiful manuscripts that people were used to buying. They even used a large initial letter at the beginning of a section, just as illuminators had done, but these letters were printed with woodblocks after the text had been printed. Here a small "a" in type showed which initial to add.

THE PRINT SHOP
Compositors and printers often worked in cramped, dark print shops. Here, the paper is delivered as the printers are inking up forms and operating the press. Finished sheets are hung up to dry around the room. The master watches with a stern eye to make sure that no one is slacking. In England a printer served an apprenticeship of at least seven years under one master before he was free to work where he chose.

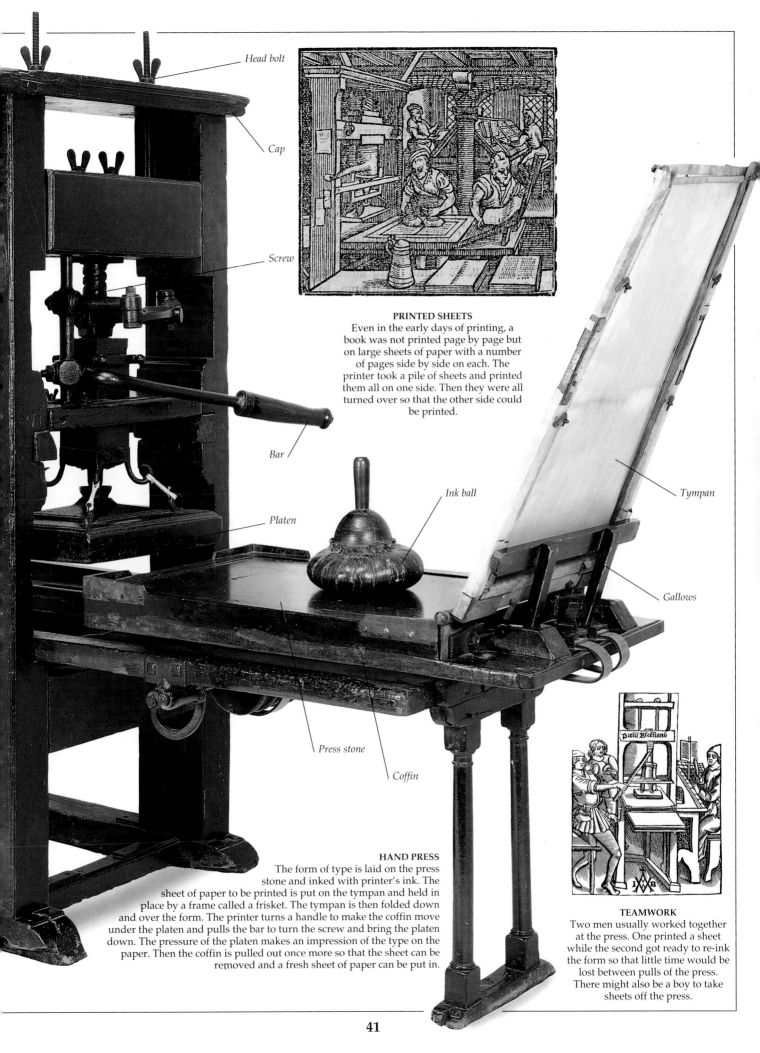

Head bolt

Cap

Screw

Bar

Platen

Press stone

Coffin

Ink ball

Tympan

Gallows

PRINTED SHEETS
Even in the early days of printing, a book was not printed page by page but on large sheets of paper with a number of pages side by side on each. The printer took a pile of sheets and printed them all on one side. Then they were all turned over so that the other side could be printed.

HAND PRESS
The form of type is laid on the press stone and inked with printer's ink. The sheet of paper to be printed is put on the tympan and held in place by a frame called a frisket. The tympan is then folded down and over the form. The printer turns a handle to make the coffin move under the platen and pulls the bar to turn the screw and bring the platen down. The pressure of the platen makes an impression of the type on the paper. Then the coffin is pulled out once more so that the sheet can be removed and a fresh sheet of paper can be put in.

TEAMWORK
Two men usually worked together at the press. One printed a sheet while the second got ready to re-ink the form so that little time would be lost between pulls of the press. There might also be a boy to take sheets off the press.

41

Early printed books

PRINTING WAS INVENTED because books, which had to be written out by hand, could not be produced quickly and cheaply enough. The first printers knew that there was a great demand for books, but also that people generally liked what they knew and often distrusted new ideas. They found ways of giving people the kind of books they were already familiar with, but in much greater numbers. The Diamond Sutra, a Chinese scroll printed with woodblocks, looks very much like a Chinese manuscript scroll. To make the first European printed books look as much as possible like manuscripts, the printers modeled their type on handwriting and even had illuminated initials and other decoration added by hand. Gradually printers introduced new typefaces, and printed books began to look more like those of today.

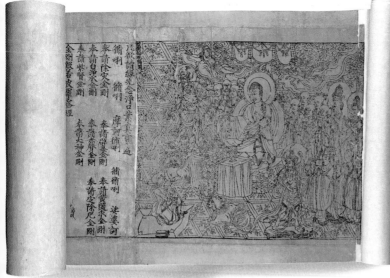

DIAMOND SUTRA

This Buddhist prayer on a scroll is thought to be the oldest complete printed book with a known publication date. It was printed in A.D. 868 using wooden blocks on seven sheets of paper glued together to form a long roll. Like many modern books, the first thing the reader sees on opening it is a picture.

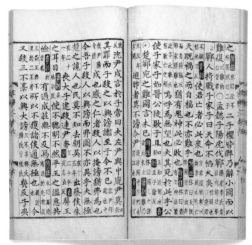

KOREAN BOOK

A Korean printer printed this book with metal type at about the same time as Johannes Gutenberg was experimenting with movable type in Germany. Casting the type for the large number of Chinese characters used by the Koreans must have taken a long time, but was one way around the shortage of wood for making woodblocks used in printing.

PRINTING IN ITALY

Printing spread rapidly from Germany to Italy, where Aldus Manutius (1449-1515) printed some of the most beautiful books of the 15th century. Each page of the story in this book is illustrated with a picture printed from a woodcut. The compositor had to put in the right number of spaces on each line to make the words form a pointed shape.

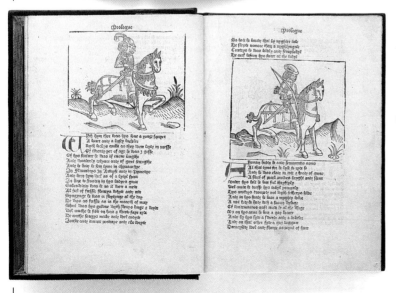

CANTERBURY TALES

William Caxton printed Geoffrey Chaucer's poem *The Canterbury Tales* in 1476 and again in 1483, when he corrected the text and added pictures. The stories of pilgrims on their way to Canterbury were very popular, and the book sold well. The type is based on the script used in Flemish books and is harder to read than the rounded letters used by Aldus Manutius.

Latin text in italic type

ITALIC TYPE

Aldus Manutius also printed books in a new type which came to be called italic because it was developed in Italy. It was modeled on the handwriting of clerks who worked in Venice. This little book by the poet Virgil was smaller and cheaper than many other printed books.

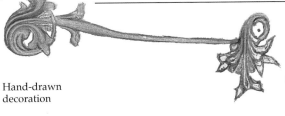

THE GUTENBERG BIBLE

Johannes Gutenberg tried out his new invention on single printed sheets before printing an entire book. In 1455, he produced the world's first printed Bible, known as the Gutenberg Bible or 42-line Bible (after the number of lines on a page). Gutenberg printed about 160 or 170 copies, some on parchment, some on paper, including this one, which is now in the British Library. It is a huge book with over 1,200 pages in two separate volumes. It probably took several years to set and print.

SPOT THE DIFFERENCE

Gutenberg wanted his printed Bible to look as much like a manuscript Bible as possible. He modeled his Gothic type on German script and laid out the page just as the scribes did. The decoration around the margins and the headings at the top of the pages were done by hand after the sheets were printed and before they were bound.

HALLMARK OF QUALITY

Most modern books give the name of the printer and the date of printing. If early printed books gave this at all it was usually at the end in a short statement called the colophon. Sometimes there was just a symbol or device which a reader would recognize. These rabbits mark the high-quality printing of Simon de Colines of Paris.

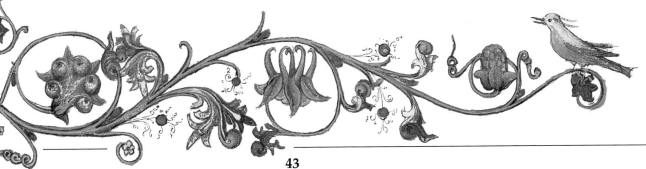

Typefaces

A TYPEFACE IS a full set of type made to a particular design. As well as being Europe's first printer, Johannes Gutenberg was also the first designer of a typeface. He had to be, because the idea of movable type was new and he was trying out his ideas in secret. Since he first made gothic type – which was modeled after German script – many other people, including famous printers, have produced designs for typefaces. Each typeface has a name – Helvetica, Palatino, Times Roman – and each has individual features. Some typefaces are suited to books, because they are clear and easy to read even in a small size. Others are too heavy for a full page of printing but make a dramatic impact when used in posters or in advertisements.

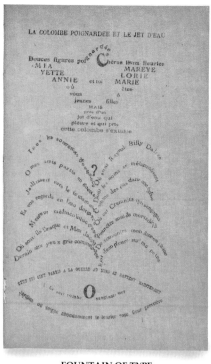

FOUNTAIN OF TYPE
Islamic calligraphy often takes the form of a bird or animal. It is much harder to do this with printed words, as type is less flexible, but this poem by French writer Guillaume Apollinaire (1880–1918) takes on the shape of its subject, a water fountain.

ABCdefg

HELVETICA
Serifs are the little cross-strokes at the end of many letters. A typeface without serifs is called a sans serif face. Helvetica is one of the most popular of this group.

ABCdefg

TIMES ROMAN
Ancient Roman carved letters had serifs, created by the sweep of the brush when letters were painted on the stone, and then chiseled out by the carver. The typeface Times Roman was designed in 1932 for the London Times newspaper and is now used very widely.

abcdefghijk

PALATINO
Typefaces with serifs, like Times Roman and Palatino, are easier to read than those without. The serifs form a link between the letters that helps to bind them together as words. This book is set in Palatino, a serif typeface created by type designer Herman Zapf.

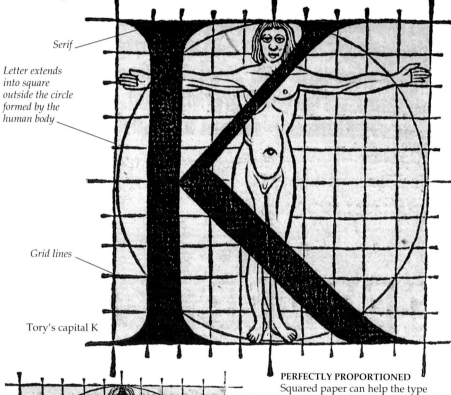

Serif

Letter extends into square outside the circle formed by the human body

Grid lines

Tory's capital K

PERFECTLY PROPORTIONED
Squared paper can help the type designer to get the proportions of a typeface correct. Geofroy Tory, a French designer of the 16th century, based these letters on the proportions of the human body. He was influenced in this by the architectural theories of the day as well as by the painter and inventor Leonardo da Vinci.

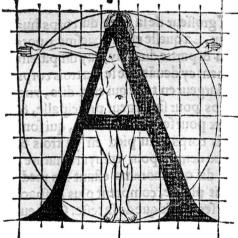

Tory's capital A

abcdefghijklmnopqrstuvwxyz

13-point Palatino roman

abcdefghijklmnopqrstuvwxyz

13-point Palatino italic

abcdefghijklmnopqrstuvwxyz

13-point Palatino bold

abcdefghijklmnopqrstuvwxyz

8-point Palatino roman

STYLES AND SIZES *left*
A typeface comes in a range of sizes, measured in units called points, and in different styles. In this book the main headings are in 36 point, introductory text is in 13 point, and captions for pictures are in 8 point. As well as the usual style, known as roman, there are also an italic and a bold style, both of which are used for emphasis.

Colour key to identify individual letters

GILL SANS
Eric Gill was a stone carver and calligrapher as well as a type designer. One of his most famous designs is the typeface Gill Sans, so called because it is a sans serif face. In his sketches for the type he has combined several letters or numbers, which are made up of the same basic shapes.

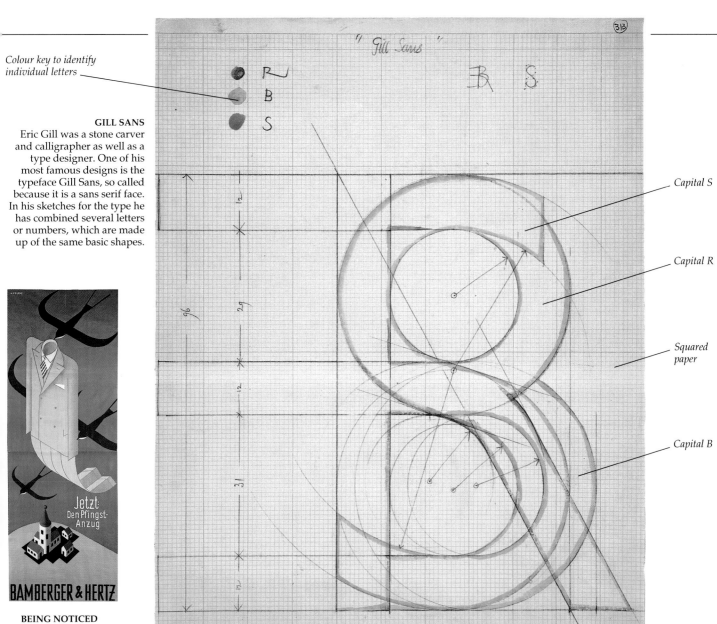

Capital S

Capital R

Squared paper

Capital B

BEING NOTICED
An advertising poster has to catch the eye of the passerby. It uses very large type that can be read easily at a distance.

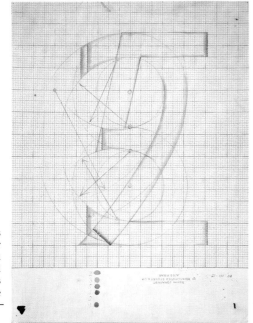

Eric Gill's designs for numbers in his Gill Sans typeface

Memorandum

FANCY FACE
All typefaces are essentially variations on the roman, gothic, or italic letter forms. In the 19th century very fancy ornate typefaces were popular, but they are not very easy to read. This one consciously echoes a medieval script.

INITIAL ILLUSTRATION
Type designers of the early 20th century sometimes combined pictures with initial letters, in imitation of medieval illuminated manuscripts (pp. 24–29).

ROMAN OR GOTHIC?
Gothic type like that made by Johannes Gutenberg was used in Germany for hundreds of years. In other countries, roman type was the standard form.

Binding

EVERY BOOK IS WRITTEN TO BE READ, but the more times a book is opened and the pages turned, the shorter its life becomes. So ever since books took the form they have today, called a codex, people have bound them to give a protective outer covering over the paper or parchment pages. This cover, or binding, can be made of wood, leather, cardboard, cloth, or even old printed sheets or manuscripts. The binding can be plain or very ornate, with decorations of gold, silver, and jewels. For the last hundred years or so most ordinary books have been bound by machine, because this is cheaper than binding by hand, but craft bookbinders still use the traditional methods developed centuries ago.

1 LOOSE SHEETS
The bookbinder receives the folded sheets of paper from the printer. These are put together in groups in the right order, ready for sewing.

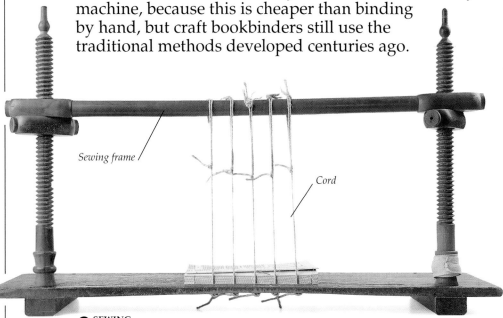

Sewing frame

Cord

2 SEWING
To hold the pages of the book together, the bookbinder sews them to cords. To do this, the cords are stretched between the top and bottom of a sewing frame. On this book, the cords will later show up as raised bands across the spine of the book. When you open a book that has been sewn in this way, it lies flat on the table without damaging the spine.

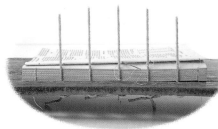

WHERE THE CORDS GO
The sewing thread passes through the fold in the section of the book, around or over the cord, and into the next section. The sections are linked together at the head or tail by a stitch called a kettle stitch.

WOMEN'S WORK?
Books have been sewn in this way in Europe for about 1,000 years. Sewing is often done by women, perhaps because their fingers are nimbler than men's, perhaps also because it fits a stereotype of women's work.

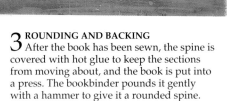

3 ROUNDING AND BACKING
After the book has been sewn, the spine is covered with hot glue to keep the sections from moving about, and the book is put into a press. The bookbinder pounds it gently with a hammer to give it a rounded spine.

Board

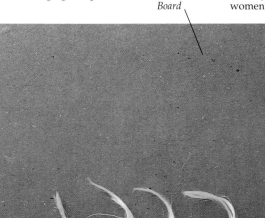

4 ATTACHING BOARDS
Now the boards which form the hard sides of the book are attached. Wooden boards were used in the Middle Ages, but today lighter materials such as pasteboard or strawboard are used. To hold the sections to the boards, the ends of the cords are drawn through holes punched in the boards and secured on the inside.

Hole in board

Raised cord

Rounded spine

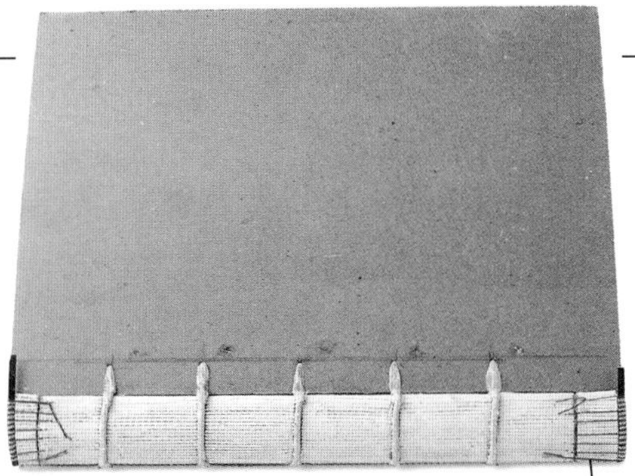

5 GIVING PROTECTION

Once the cords have been secured and the boards are firmly in place, a headband and tailband can be added to protect the book when it is opened. The book is now ready to be covered.

Colored tailband

Brown cloth

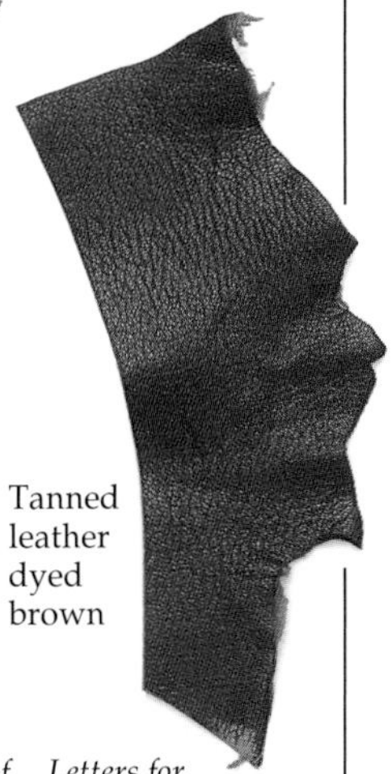

Tanned leather dyed brown

Nippers for making the raised band

Raised band

Wooden screw press to hold book steady

6 COVERING

This book is covered in cloth with leather corners and spine to give extra protection to the most vulnerable parts. The cloth and leather are pasted onto the boards and turned over the edges to the inside.

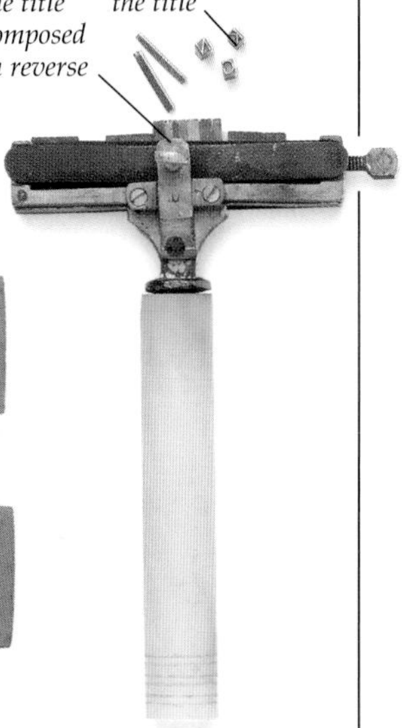

Words of the title composed in reverse   *Letters for the title*

Gold-tooled rose

Gold-tooled crown

Typeholder

7 FINISHING TOUCHES

The book is now ready to have the spine decorated. The binder paints the spine with glair (egg white) and lays the gold leaf on it. Heated tools are used to press the design through the gold onto the leather. Then the binder rubs off the surplus gold.

Gold leaf

8 THE BOUND BOOK

The finished book is attractive to look at and will last a long time.

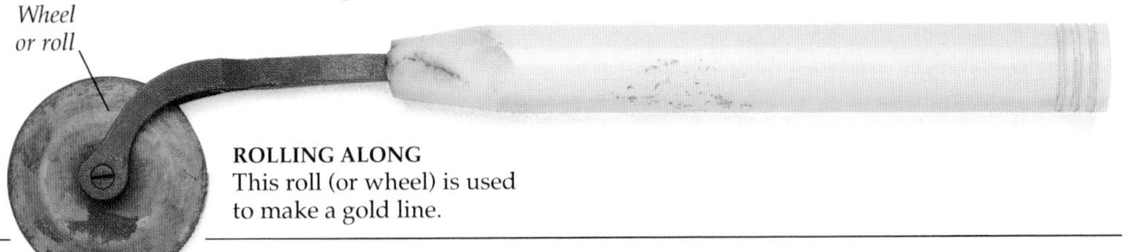

TRADITIONAL TECHNIQUES

Two hundred years ago binders used the same kind of equipment they use today. Here they are applying gold leaf to the edges of pages and using a roll to make lines.

Tools for impressing the rose, crown, and lines on the spine

Wheel or roll

ROLLING ALONG

This roll (or wheel) is used to make a gold line.

Illustrated books

PICTURES HAVE ALWAYS been used in books, either to add information or to make the text more attractive. Perhaps the first illustrated books were the ancient Egyptian Books of the Dead, long papyrus rolls with pictures and hieroglyphs. Illuminated manuscripts were the illustrated books of the Middle Ages, and the first printers imitated them by using woodcuts. Medieval manuscripts are magnificent because of their brightly colored pictures and decorated letters. But in early printed books the color usually had to be added by hand after printing. In the 19th century, new technology made color printing possible.

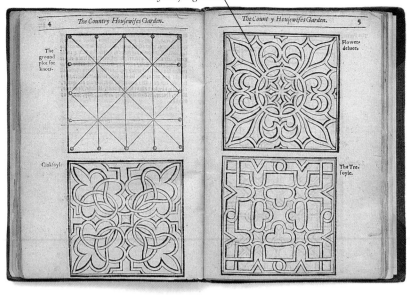

Woodcut showing planting layout for garden

COUNTRY GARDENS

Many practical books would be difficult to understand without illustrations. Printers soon began to combine text and illustrations, just as scribes had done before them. Illustrations were carved into pieces of wood to create blocks from which the pictures could be printed. Such illustrations are called woodcuts. This gardening manual, illustrated with woodcuts, appeared in 1618.

WHAT'S IT ALL ABOUT?

A picture on the title page of a book usually tells the reader what the book is about. This couple appear on the title page of a book of anonymous folk songs published in Germany in 1560. To keep costs down, early printers often re-used woodcuts in different books. Sometimes the pictures had nothing to do with the text!

FAIRY TALES

The role of pictures in medieval manuscripts and in modern books is often simply to illustrate the story. An illuminated manuscript like Froissart's Chronicle (pp. 28–29) and this Russian fairy-tale book, published in 1901, have many features in common. Illustrator Ivan Bilbibin drew these pictures for the story of Prince Ivan, the Firebird, and the Gray Wolf.

Border detail from the book of Russian fairy tales

WORKS OF ART
Modern artists who are well known for work in other fields often collaborate with writers to produce illustrated books. This illustration to a poem by the French writer Guillaume Apollinaire is by Raoul Dufy (1877–1953).

COLOR PLATES *above*
In the 19th century, illustrations were often printed from engravings made on steel plates. The pictures were printed on different sheets of paper from the text. Costume books, like this one describing army uniforms, were especially popular.

Detail of dragon from the news sheet

STRANGE EVENTS
left and right
Today's newspapers rely heavily on photographs to catch the reader's attention and to give the atmosphere of a story. In the 16th century, a news sheet like this used a picture in exactly the same way. This example is a translation into German of a report of extraordinary happenings in Navarre (in modern Spain), including the appearance of strange creatures. For added impact, the most dramatic events have been picked out in color by hand after printing.

LOOK CLOSER
By 1905, when this illustration was produced, the range of illustrated books was enormous. A good illustration can make the reader stop and look hard at what is on the page.

Learning words

WRITING IS NO LONGER a special skill practiced only by highly trained scribes. To survive in the modern world, everyone needs to be able to write. The invention of printing did much to encourage the skill of writing. Printing made books available to more people than could have afforded manuscripts, and readily available books made people want to be able to read and write as well. In the 19th century, the introduction of postal services brought an increase in letter-writing, and written communication grew rapidly. In countries where schooling is compulsory for every child, there is no longer a barrier to universal literacy – the idea that every person should be able to read and write.

BETWEEN THE LINES
An essential part of learning to write is copying the shapes of letters until you can write them with ease. About 1,800 years ago a pupil made two attempts to copy these lines of Greek from the master's writing at the top. In spite of the parallel lines the pupil's writing was not very neat. Perhaps it was just as well that this was a wax tablet, which allowed the pupil to rub out the letters and start again.

Wooden spelling board

IN CLASS
The classroom of the past was a much stricter place than the schools of today. Children spent a lot of time listening to the teacher and learning by heart. The children who attended this 19th-century school were given a free education, although many parents had to pay in this period.

Wooden box

SPELL IT OUT
Learning to spell can be a chore, especially in languages with complicated spelling rules. Items like this 19th-century wooden spelling board could help.

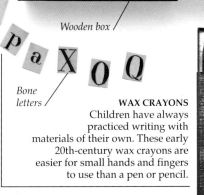

Bone letters

WAX CRAYONS
Children have always practiced writing with materials of their own. These early 20th-century wax crayons are easier for small hands and fingers to use than a pen or pencil.

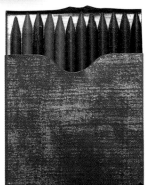

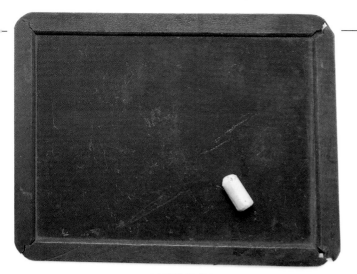

SAFEKEEPING
Scribes have always looked after their pens and brushes, carefully keeping them in special cases. Pencil cases come in many shapes and sizes. This wooden pencil box in the shape of a book is three hundred years old.

Compass for drawing circles

ON THE SLATE
A hundred years ago children copied letters onto slates with a piece of chalk or a slate pencil. This was not very different from the wax tablets of ancient Greece or Rome.

Chancery script

Paper covered with transparent animal horn

BOOK IN THE HAND
A hornbook, used for learning to read, gets its name from the sheet of horn covering the paper on which the words are printed. It keeps sticky fingers from making marks on the paper.

Handle for child to hold while reading text

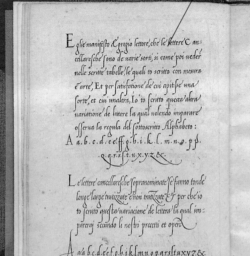

PRACTICE MAKES PERFECT
For hundreds of years, books have been written which teach the art of calligraphy (pp. 6–7). Over 400 years ago, the Venetian writing master Giovanni Tagliente produced this book. The style of writing shown, called Chancery script, was the basis of the italic type used in printing in Italy (pp. 42–43). The letters in the book are not written, but printed from a woodblock.

HIS NIBS
Once they could form the letters properly, children started to use a pen. By the 19th century metal nibs had replaced quill pens.

INK FOR ALL
Every classroom needed inkwells, which when not in use were stored on a tray like this.

51

KING'S MARK
Many medieval rulers could not read or write. Instead of signing his name on this official order William I, king of England (1027–1087), made the sign of a cross, as did his wife Matilda. Later their names were written beside the crosses by someone else.

Handwriting

LIKE A FINGERPRINT, everyone's handwriting is unique. No two people write in exactly the same way, even if they were taught to write by the same teacher. As people grow up, their handwriting changes and matures, and they can learn to write in a different style if they want to. This makes it difficult for one person to imitate another's writing accurately. The way you write also depends on the materials you use as well as on the purpose of the writing. A scribbled shopping list, a school composition, and a formal letter written by the same person will look very different. Different writing styles have also been used in different periods. Analyzing handwriting for what it reveals about a person's character is called graphology.

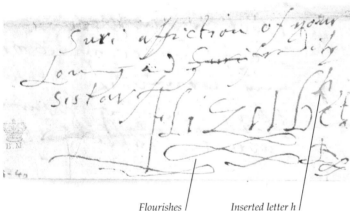

RENAISSANCE WRITING
The artist Michelangelo (1475–1564) had a typical 16th-century Italian (or italic) style of writing. People still write in an italic hand today, for which they need a special pen with a slanting nib.

ROYAL FLOURISH
Elizabeth I of England (1533-1603) had an impressive signature with many cross-strokes and flourishes. It could be the reflection of a vain person or it could be an attempt to prevent anyone from forging her signature. Here she has not left enough room for all her name and has had to put the last letter on the line above.

Flourishes | Inserted letter h

MIRROR WRITING
One way to make it difficult for others to read your handwriting is to write in reverse. Leonardo da Vinci (1452-1519), the Italian artist and inventor, made notes on his scientific experiments in mirror writing like this.

QUEEN'S SIGNATURE
Marie Antoinette (1755–1793), the wife of Louis XVI of France, was executed during the French Revolution. By studying many examples of her signature and her handwriting a graphologist may be able to tell what sort of person she was.

George Washington

18th-century inkstand

PRESIDENTIAL HANDWRITING
George Washington (1732–1799) was the first president of the United States. His signature has many flourishes and looks quite impressive. People in public life may have two different signatures, one for official papers and one for private letters.

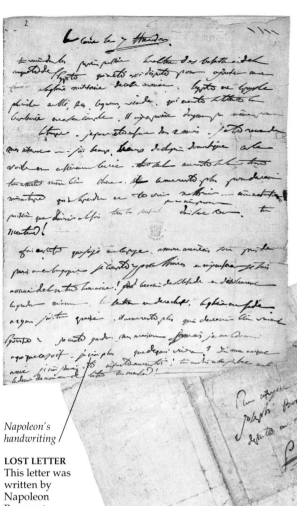

Napoleon Bonaparte

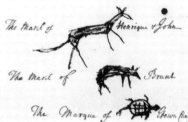

ANIMAL MARKS
A signature is a way of identifying yourself and showing agreement. These 19th-century native North American signatures take the form of drawings of animals.

Napoleon's handwriting

LOST LETTER
This letter was written by Napoleon Bonaparte (1769–1821) to his brother Joseph in 1798 but was never delivered. The courier who was carrying it was intercepted and the letter was found by English admiral Lord Nelson, who added a note. In the 19th century letters were not put into envelopes but were folded and sealed with wax.

Wax seal

Lord Nelson's handwriting

GANDHI
Old letters can turn out to be very valuable, especially if they were written by someone who later became famous. The Indian leader Mahatma Gandhi (1869–1948), wrote this note in 1914, while in South Africa.

Steel nibbed pen

NIBS
Steel nibs took over from the quill pen in the 19th century; both were slow to write with, as they had to be dipped into ink every few seconds. The fountain pen transformed writing – it holds a supply of ink in its reservoir and allows just enough to flow down to the nib.

FINE WRITING
Calligraphers (pp. 6–7) produce handwriting that is also art. This is a piece of 19th-century calligraphy from Iran. The writing is on marbled paper.

MASTER'S ROLL
In the 16th and 17th centuries there was great interest in developing elegant handwriting, and there were many famous writing masters. This is a Russian writing master's roll showing Cyrillic script in a style with many flourishes.

Quill pen

Fountain pen

Children's books

TODAY, CHILDREN HAVE a huge choice of books to read for pleasure, but this has not always been the case. For hundreds of years there were no books written specially for children, who, if they could read at all, had to make do with books written for adults. Later there were school books to teach grammar and spelling, and moral tales to teach them how to behave properly. About 250 years ago publishers began to produce alphabet books, rhymes, and fairy tales for children, and gradually this led to adventure stories, animal stories, and the other kinds of children's books we have today.

Place thumb here

Strings to hold moving parts together

MOVING PICTURES
Books with pictures that move and change are always popular. In this tale of an old sugar tub the picture stands out from the page as you open the book, and the dog appears to swim toward you.

CLOTH BOOK
Books for very small children are sometimes printed on cloth rather than paper, because cloth is much stronger. This one shows a selection of everyday objects that the child can recognize.

Pictures printed on cloth

Pop-up letter W

POP-UP
When you open this book flat on a table, the letters and objects spring up off the page and stand up straight. The book shows each letter of the alphabet and how to write it as a capital and small letter. Movable books first appeared in the 19th century. This type of pop-up book was very popular about 60 years ago.

W for Windmill
in a meadow close by
X is the letter
that's standing next to Y
Y is for Yacht
that is not pronounced yacht
Z is for Zebra
the last of the batch.

THE REAL ALICE
At the end of the manuscript of *Alice's Adventures in Wonderland*, Lewis Carroll included a picture of Alice Liddell, the little girl who had inspired him. She was associated with the book throughout her life.

ALICE AND THE DODO
Lewis Carroll did not think that his own drawings were good enough to be used when the story was published in 1865. Instead, the cartoonist John Tenniel was asked to illustrate the work. Here is his idea of what the Dodo looked like.

DANCERS
Children in European countries could read about Alice's adventures in their own language soon after children in England. Here a Dutch Alice is watching the Gryphon and the Mock Turtle dance the Lobster Quadrille.

WHITE RABBIT
Many different artists since Tenniel have illustrated the Alice stories. Here a fashionable Alice from the 1920s meets the elegant White Rabbit, who is so startled by her that he drops his gloves and fan.

than she expected: before she had drunk half the bottle, she found her head pressing against the ceiling, and she stooped to save her neck from being broken, and hastily put down the bottle, saying to herself "that's quite enough—I hope I shan't grow any more—I wish I hadn't drunk so much!" Alas! it was too late: she went on growing and growing, and very soon had to kneel down: in another minute there was not room even for this, and she tried the effect of lying down, with one elbow against the door, and the other arm curled round her head. Still she went on growing, and as a last resource she put one arm out of the window, and one foot up the chimney, and said to herself "now I can do no more—what *will* become of me?"

ALICE IN WONDERLAND
Alice's Adventures in Wonderland began life as a story told by Lewis Carroll (1832-1898), a young Oxford University professor, to some children on a river trip in 1862. Later he wrote it out neatly with drawings as a present for one of the children, Alice Liddell. The original manuscript is now kept in the British Library, London.

ALICE AND THE MOUSE *right*
Nearly everyone's idea of Alice is a little girl with long blond hair, but sometimes she is shown looking more like the real Alice Liddell, who had short, dark hair with bangs.

THE CHESHIRE CAT
Lewis Carroll's animals are a mixture of his vivid imagination and the features of his friends. Alice looks puzzled by a cat that grins at her from a tree.

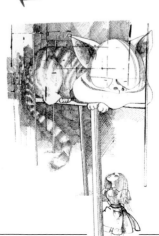

A NEW NAME
Alice's Adventures in Wonderland has been translated into almost every language, including the invented language Esperanto. There is even a shorthand version. This is Alice from an edition in the African language Swahili, in which she is called Elisi.

Words at work

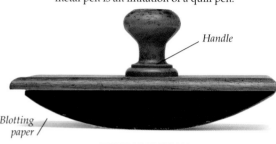

FALSE FEATHER
Medieval scribes wrote with a quill pen made from a hardened feather of a large bird. Metal nibs came into common use in the 1830s. This metal pen is an imitation of a quill pen.

THE FIRST WRITING was probably used for accounting and record-keeping (pp. 8–9), and writing has been vital in all sorts of workplaces ever since. The first merchants needed lists of their goods and accounts of their business deals; governments needed to keep records of where people lived and what they owned, so that they could collect taxes. People who could read and write were therefore important and valued members of society, particularly because few had these skills before the 19th century. By that time, with the huge growth of industry and the rise in population, armies of clerks were employed to write everything down by hand. With the advent of the typewriter (pp. 58–59), there was a large change in office life.

Handle

Blotting paper

KEEPING IT CLEAN
A blotter was essential for preventing smudges of ink on the paper. In this example, the blotting paper is stretched around the curved surface of the blotter. The writer gently rocks the blotter back and forth over the wet ink.

SCRIVENERS' KNIVES
Scribes needed knives, like these two from the 17th century, for cutting pieces of parchment or paper and for preparing quills. To make a quill, the scribe had to trim away part of the feather to make a shaft that was comfortable to hold. Then the tip of the feather was cut to the scribe's preferred shape and a slit was made, so that the pen would hold the ink.

OPENING UP
Envelopes for letters were introduced in the 19th century. Today a busy office receives hundreds of letters every day. The easiest way to open them is to slit the top with a paper knife. Many paper knives have elaborately decorated ends.

AT THE OFFICE
This office is typical of the late 19th century. The clerk, who has a pen tucked behind his ear so that he does not mislay it, keeps all the correspondence in files in a cupboard. On his desk are his writing tools. Today paper files are being replaced by records kept on a computer.

ORGANIZER
Office workers are always looking for ways of keeping their desks tidy and well organized. Wooden racks like this one were popular in the early 20th century for holding letters and stationery.

Early 20th-century ink bottle

STEPHENS'
BLUE BLACK
WRITING FLUID

ON THE RECORD

Record-keeping has always been one of the most important uses of writing at work. This 19th-century view shows part of Somerset House, London, a large building which housed the British records of births, marriages, and deaths. Today, records of this type can be kept on computer, where they take up much less space.

SIGNED AND SEALED

In the 15th century, a business agreement looked like this. It was written out by hand and sealed with wax to show that all parties agreed. This document records the transfer of a shop and all its contents from one trader to another in 1407.

Wax seal

QUILLS

Feathers from a large bird, like a goose, make the best quill pens. Because of the way they curve, feathers from the left wing suit a righthanded person and vice versa. This ink pot and quill pens are from the 17th century.

Goose-feather quill

RAPID WRITING

Shorthand is a way of writing very quickly using symbols or abbreviations instead of the usual letters of the alphabet. The ancient Greeks and Romans developed a kind of shorthand, but it did not last. In 1837 Isaac Pitman invented this system, which uses dots, dashes, and straight and curved lines. It is still widely used, especially for dictated letters.

A HIGH PERCH

In the 19th century, clerks usually sat on tall stools and worked at sloping desks like this. The slope was supposed to make writing easier, but the slouching posture of this clerk makes it look rather uncomfortable.

EMBOSSER

This device provides a way of stamping a name or address on to paper or business cards. A sheet of paper is inserted, and when you pull the handle, the machine embosses the words on to the paper so that they stand up in relief.

The typewriter

SEVERAL INVENTORS experimented with "writing machines" of various kinds before William Austin Burt, an American, produced the first typewriter – made entirely of wood – in 1829. The writing machines were often slower than writing by hand, but in 1867 another American, Christopher Latham Scholes, produced the first efficient machine. Typewriters were slow to catch on in offices because clerks were cheap to employ and produced neat handwritten documents. But eventually typewriters became standard office equipment and replaced clerks altogether. The first typewriters were large and heavy, with hundreds of moving parts. In the early 20th century an electric typewriter was developed; it took the hard work out of typing. Portable typewriters meant that journalists covering a major story could type it up right away. Today the typewriter is being replaced by the word processor.

STANDARD MODEL
The first commercially produced typewriter in the world was sold by the Remington Company in 1873. By the early 20th century, the Remington Standard looked like this, a heavy, solidly built machine that was found in hundreds of offices all over the world.

TYPISTS
Typing is a very useful skill for all kinds of work. The American writer Mark Twain (1835–1910) was probably the first author to send a typescript to his publisher. By the middle of the 20th century, offices everywhere relied on typists for letter-writing and record-keeping.

Paper rest

Bell

Rods to link keys to type bars

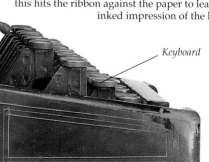

Carriage-return lever

MANUAL MECHANISM
All the parts of a manual typewriter are linked together mechanically. There are about 2,000 parts in all. The typist feeds in a sheet of paper at the back of the machine and turns a knob to bring it up around the front of the roller, or platen, to the right position to be struck by the type bars. As the typist hits a key on the keyboard, a series of mechanical linking rods makes one of the type bars pop up. Each bar has a small metal letter in reverse on its end, and this hits the ribbon against the paper to leave an inked impression of the letter.

Keyboard

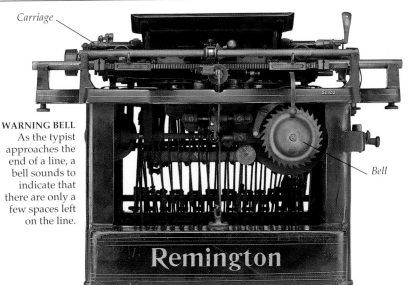

Carriage

WARNING BELL
As the typist approaches the end of a line, a bell sounds to indicate that there are only a few spaces left on the line.

Bell

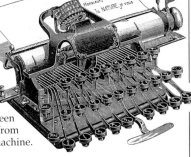

ANOTHER LAYOUT
Typewriters in many countries use the QWERTY keyboard layout, but numerous other keyboards have been tried. This one is from an early French machine.

ABCDEFGHIJKLMNOPQRSTUVWXYZ
abcdefghijklmnopqrstuvwxyz

EEEEEEEEEEEEEEEEEEEEEEEEE
WWWWWWWWWWWWWWWWWWWWWW

EQUAL SPACES
Unlike type for printing, where individual letters have different widths, all the letters on a typewriter occupy the same space. On a manual typewriter, the appearance of the letters is affected by how heavily you strike the keys, which can give an uneven look to the typing.

Platen

Paper gauge

Type bars

These keys give QWERTY keyboard its name

CARRIAGE RETURNS
The carriage moves along with each stroke of a key. At the end of the line the typist must pull the carriage-return lever to move the paper up and the carriage back before typing the next line. The carriage moves in the same direction as the direction of handwriting, so in a Hebrew or Arabic typewriter it moves from right to left.

KEYBOARD
The earliest "writing machines" had keyboards like a piano, with one long bank of letters in alphabetical order. When the typist was typing quite fast, the keys that were used most often became jammed. This led to the development of the QWERTY keyboard, which reduces jamming and is still in use today. By pressing the shift key, the typist can instantly change from small letters to capitals.

The book market

BOOKS ARE BIG BUSINESS and always have been. In the Middle Ages monks were so keen to get hold of manuscripts to copy that they even borrowed them from foreign monasteries. Once printing was established in Europe, the real trade in books began with printers selling their own books. Later on printers usually worked for a publisher, who distributed books to bookshops, which in turn sold them to the customer. Today, books are sold everywhere from airports to supermarkets. The best-selling book ever is probably the Bible, which has been published in over 800 languages. William Shakespeare is probably the world's best-selling author.

MEDIEVAL BOOKSHOP
When all books had to be written by hand, it was not possible just to go into a bookshop, pick a book off the shelf to buy, and take it home to read. Students had to pay to borrow books from the university bookshop to copy out for themselves.

TRAVELING SALESMAN
By the 15th century, there were bookstores – often run by printers – in the big towns. ABCs and religious books for the ordinary people were sold by hawkers who went from place to place selling their wares.

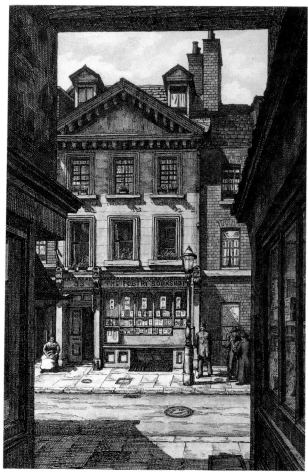

TEMPLE OF THE MUSES
James Lackington made a fortune selling books at very low prices in his London shop in the 18th century. He was probably the first person to sell remainders – books that are flops and do not sell at full price.

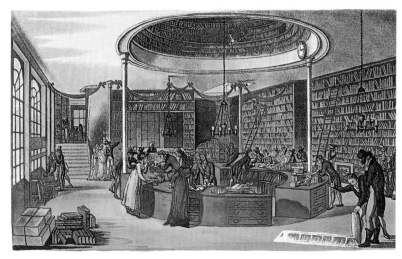

LARGE AND SMALL
Bookstores come in all shapes and sizes, from the grand to the tiny and cramped, like this 18th-century one with books piled high everywhere.

STORES OF ALL TYPES
Some bookstores specialize in just one subject – this one sold only poetry books. Others are proud of being able to get any book currently in print within a day or two. There is also a big trade in second-hand books, especially among book collectors. Very rare old books are sold at special auctions and can command high prices.

Gold leaf

Leather

THE ROLE OF THE PUBLISHER
Publishers are a powerful link in the book chain: they decide which books to publish and how much they should cost. The publisher can be recognized by a logo like this which appears on the jackets and spines.

BOOK SMUGGLERS
Publishing is an international business. The German firm of Tauchnitz published more than 6,500 books by British and American authors and sold more than 40 million copies worldwide. For copyright reasons it was illegal to bring these cheap English-language editions into Britain, but many travelers hid them in the linings of their coats and staggered past customs weighed down by all their books.

FINE BINDING
Originally books were sold unbound. After you had bought a book, you went to a bookbinder and ordered a binding to suit your taste and pocket. Today most books are either machine-bound hardcovers or paperbacks. Bookbinders do still make individual bindings for fine books, like this volume of French poetry. However, such books are often collected as objects to be admired rather as than books to be read.

ON BOARD
Traveling bookselling went on into the 20th century in many countries, with vans like this going out from major cities into the Italian countryside.

Publisher's logo

PAPERBACKS
About one-third of all books sold today are paperbacks. They are often so popular that they have to be reprinted many times. Paperbacks have made books available to everyone because they are cheap and handy. These are the first Penguins, popular paperbacks sold in English-speaking countries, which first appeared in 1935. Paperbacks soon followed in other countries.

Keeping your words

THE FIRST LIBRARIES were great storehouses in Babylonia and ancient Egypt that contained records written on clay tablets or papyrus rolls. In the Middle Ages, when books were rare and precious, a book chest or a cupboard was often large enough to contain a collection of books. Only the libraries of big churches and universities had more than a few hundred volumes. Even after printing made books more widely available and more people learned to read, libraries were still open only to the rich. By the 18th century there were libraries in Europe that people could pay to use, but not until the 20th century was there a free public library service in most countries.

ALEXANDRIA
One of the most famous libraries of the ancient world was at Alexandria in Egypt. Scholars and scientists came from all over the Greek-speaking world to study there and to add to the library's collections by translating and copying more texts. At one time it is said to have contained more than 400,000 works on papyrus rolls stored on shelves, each with a label to identify it.

Theology and philosophy

Catalog of the books

Poetry

Small book bound in parchment

Ribbon to keep book closed

TRAVELING LIBRARY
Sir Julius Caesar, a 16th-century English judge, owned this unusual traveling library of 44 small books, each bound in parchment with gold tooling. Books on theology and philosophy are on the top shelf; history is in the middle; poetry is on the bottom shelf. The outside of the box is covered in leather to make it look like a book.

CHAINED UP
Books are portable and often disappear from libraries. To prevent this from happening in the medieval library at Hereford Cathedral in England, the books were chained to a rod along the bookcase. The chains were attached to the front covers, so the books were shelved with their spines to the back.

SILENCE, PLEASE
A library is an essential part of every school and university. In the past no talking was allowed in the library so that students could concentrate on their books. Nowadays a school library will be alive with the hum of computers and children working together on projects.

PAY AS YOU READ
Before public libraries existed, people had to pay to borrow books from a private library. There were libraries for gentlemen in the 18th century and subscription libraries in the 19th century. Private libraries were especially popular in seaside and spa towns, where visitors had free time for reading. This one was at Margate on the English coast.

READING HABITS
At the beginning of the 20th century reading was the most popular source of entertainment, but today reading is a less popular hobby than watching television. Libraries have had to change to meet people's needs, so they now stock records, tapes, and even videos as well as books.

NATIONAL STOREHOUSE
The British Library in London is one of the world's largest libraries. It contains not just books and manuscripts but also newspapers, maps, music, sound recordings, and stamps. The books alone cover more than 206 miles (332 km) of shelves, mostly in the form of book stacks to which readers are not admitted – if you want a book, it is brought from the stack to a desk in a reading room. By law the Library receives a copy of every new book published in Britain.

BOOKS ON WHEELS
A mobile library brings books to people who live too far from town to visit the library. In the 19th century, working people could get books from this kind of horse-drawn mobile library.

Index

Acknowledgments

Dorling Kindersley would like to thank:

The following members of the British Library staff for their assistance: Jane Carr, David Way, Kathy Houghton, Alan Sterenberg, Ann de Lara, Angela Roach, Janet Benoy, Frances Ash-Glover, Janet Backhouse, Michelle Brown, Scot McKendrick, Andrew Prescott, Julian Conway, Mike Boggan and the staff of the Department of Manuscripts Photographic Administration, Frances Wood, Yu-Ying Brown, Yasin Safadi, Brad Sabin Hill, Jerry Losty, Muhammed Isa Waley, Annabel Gallop, Patricia Herbert, Henry Ginsberg, Linda Raymond, Peter Lawson, Chris Thomas, David Paisey, John Barr, Elizabeth James, John Goldfinch, Marcella Leembruggen, Graham Jefcoate, Geoff West, Philippa Marks, Mike Western, Roy Russell, Brian Russell, Ken Roullier, and Graham Marsh. We would also like to thank the following for help: John Hutchinson, Anna Kruger, Jabu Mahlangu, Gavin Morgan, James Mosley, Andrew Nash, Jim Rain, and David Sinfield; and Nick Nicolls and Peter Hayman of The British Museum for additional special photography.
The author would also like to thank Barbara Brend for checking text.

Picture credits
a=above, b=below, c=center, l=left, r=right, t=top
Ancient Art & Architecture Collection: 8tl, 10cl
Staatsbibliothek Bamberg: 21tl
Biblioteca Universitaria de Bologna/ Photo:Rongaglia: 21lc
Bridgeman Art Library/British Museum: 8c; /Louvre Paris: 12bl; /Trinity College Cambridge: 26tr; /Bibliothèque Nationale Paris: 27tr; /Bodleian Library: 51lc; /Fine Art Society: 60br; /City of Edinburgh Museum & Art Gallery: 60bc, 63 tr
Camera Press: 10bc
E. T. Archive: 29bl, 45tl, 45br
Mary Evans Picture Library: 7tr, 31lc, 38br, 39rc, 49bl, 57bl, 57tr, 60cl, 61bl, 62tr, 63c, 63bl
Paul Felix: 7bc

Vivien Fifield: 59tr
Fotomas Index: 63cl
Robert Harding Picture Library: 13cl, 14tr, 18lc, 20cl, 34c
Michael Holford: 13tr
Peter Newark's Pictures: 36tl, 39lc, 41br, 50rc
Pitkin Pictorials: 63tl
Stapleton Collection: 23t, 23c, 37cr, 49tr, 52bc, 60bl
St Bride Printing Library: 45tr, 45bl
ZEFA: 7c

Every effort has been made to trace the copyright holders and we apologise in advance for any uninentional omissions. We would be pleased to insert the appropriate acknowledgement in any subsequent edition of this publication.

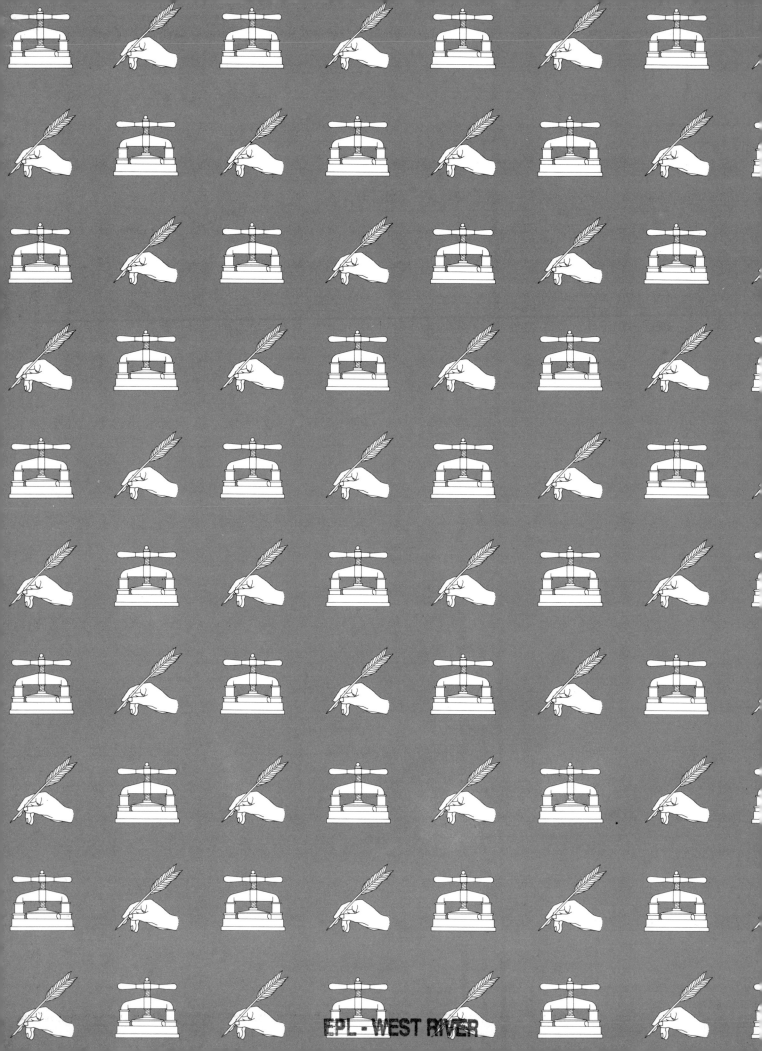